Perfect Game USA
and the Future of Baseball

Perfect Game USA and the Future of Baseball

How the Remaking of Youth Scouting Affects the National Pastime

LES EDGERTON

Foreword by Wally Lubanski

McFarland & Company, Inc., Publishers
Jefferson, North Carolina, and London

All photographs are by the author unless otherwise credited.

Library of Congress Cataloguing-in-Publication Data

Edgerton, Leslie.
  Perfect Game USA and the future of baseball : how the
remaking of youth scouting affects the national pastime /
Les Edgerton ; foreword by Wally Lubanski.
      p.   cm.
  Includes bibliographical references and index.

  ISBN 978-0-7864-3408-4
  softcover : 50# alkaline paper ∞

  1. Baseball for children.   2. Baseball — Scouting.   I. Title.
GV880.4.E34   2009
796.357'62 — dc22   2008041581

British Library cataloguing data are available

Cover photograph ©2008 Shutterstock

Manufactured in the United States of America

*McFarland & Company, Inc., Publishers
  Box 611, Jefferson, North Carolina 28640
  www.mcfarlandpub.com*

To my kids, Britney, Sienna and Mike,
who are each my favorite.

To my wife, Mary, who is,
to use a baseball term,
a five-tool wife and scores an 80 on the 20–80 scale.

Acknowledgments

First and above all others, I owe a tremendous debt of gratitude to the founder, chief architect, and guiding light of Perfect Game USA, Jerry Ford himself. Without his generosity of spirit, this book would never have been able to come into existence. The same applies to his wife, Betty, and to all the members of the Perfect Game organization, many of whom I should have written about here, but simply didn't have enough space.

I owe much to the students who helped me conduct dozens of interviews. Special thanks to Mike Leyland and Chris Wells, my students when I taught at the University of Toledo, who volunteered their services in conducting interviews for the book. And, yes; Mike is related to Detroit Tigers' manager Jim Leyland — Jim is his uncle. There's a funny story about how he and I connected for this project.

I was given very gracious permission by the university to use students who could earn independent study credit to assist me in my research. After I announced the opportunity in my classes, a young man approached to inquire if I'd consider him for the project. This was the second class Mike Leyland had taken from me, but I'd never figured out that he was related to the Detroit Tigers' skipper. That was because I thought Mike's name was pronounced "Lay-land" and he'd never corrected me when I'd called on him and used that pronunciation. There were two other reasons I didn't make the connection. One, I didn't realize that the Leyland clan was from the nearby town of Perrysburg. The second reason I didn't know who Mike was related to was that I didn't follow the American League much because for years I've refused to acknowledge they even still played baseball in the Junior Circuit. Why? Because of that designated hitter monstrosity. I've been a bitter enemy of the rule ever since it came into existence. All I'll say is that most of the AL hitting records should be marked with an asterisk, in my opinion.

Well, since Mike and I began to work together, I've since learned that not only does he look, talk, and walk like his famous uncle, he's got the same

viii   Acknowledgments

work ethic. His help has been immense, and I thank him from the bottom of
my heart.

When I moved to teach at Tri-State University in Angola, Indiana, I asked for student volunteers who might be interested in helping me conduct research. I hit the mother lode! My wonderful "crew" of very able research assistants and interviewers includes the following downright terrific people: Omar A. Hosani, Mitch Harshbarger, Cliff Meyer, Joe Clark, Derek Brenneman, Sam Clinton, Kara L. Benschneider, Stephen Kahl, Jake Colson, Mario Ramon, Brenton Barteck, and Dan Higginbotham. I can't thank you folks enough — you're the greatest!

Table of Contents

Foreword
by Wally Lubanski

Opportunity.

Webster defines the word, in part, as "a good chance or occasion, as to advance oneself." In the amateur baseball world, few organizations promote the spirit of opportunity as well as Perfect Game USA. For literally thousands of young players striving to realize their potential on the baseball diamond, Perfect Game USA has provided the unique opportunity — the vehicle — for these players to demonstrate their tools and talent to baseball decision-makers from coast to coast. By developing a very broad, expanding stage for up-and-coming prospects to "show their stuff," Perfect Game USA has played an enormous role in helping to fulfill the dreams of many players.

My family's relationship with Perfect Game USA began in January 2001, when my oldest son, Chris, attended his first Perfect Game event, the World Showcase, in Fort Myers, Florida. Just a sophomore in high school at the time, Chris competed at the national event with players from across the country, many of them older and with much more impressive baseball resumes than he had. Hailing from Schewenksville, Pennsylvania — not exactly a traditional baseball hotbed — Chris took a huge leap from the comfortable confines of the local baseball surroundings at home.

Although a dose of Florida weather certainly beats a bleak, frigid Pennsylvania winter any day of the week, Chris' first baseball experience in the Sunshine State began with uncertainty and, frankly, a little apprehension, too. After all, Chris was now playing with and against some of the finest baseball talent in the country ... the cream of the crop! How would a skinny kid from a cold weather state stack up against the best that amateur baseball had to offer? Would Chris' first encounter with Perfect Game be his last? Was this Perfect Game opportunity worth the time and expense — or should Chris simply depend on that baseball adage, "If you are good enough, they will find you," essentially limiting his baseball pursuits to his own backyard, thus rolling the dice in the hope of maybe being discovered by a college recruiter or pro scout?

Chris learned a ton at that first Perfect Game showcase — the feedback he obtained from Perfect Game was invaluable in helping him understand the areas of the game he needed to improve upon, a key to his future development. Chris further benefited by gaining big-time showcase experience at a relatively young age, experience that would only help him later as his journey progressed. He was now on the baseball radar as well, as Perfect Game began to develop a player profile on Chris, data that could be relied upon later by college programs and major league clubs. Moreover, Chris took full advantage of his moment in the sun, competing successfully with a caliber of talent that he would not routinely come across on his home turf.

The feedback, the exposure, the competition ... all of it helped to motivate Chris to continue developing his passion and talent. He faced the challenge — the opportunity — that Perfect Game provided, and he rose to the occasion. As they say, the rest is history. Chris went on to compete in numerous Perfect Game showcases and tournaments, locally, regionally, and nation-

The Lubanski brothers — from left, Joe, Mike and Chris — have all participated in Perfect Game events. In June 2003, Chris became the first-round draft pick of the Kansas City Royals, the No. 5 pick in the nation, and signed with the Royals for a $2.1 million bonus (courtesy Wally Lubanski).

ally. The skinny kid from Pennsylvania would play for two summers with the USA Baseball National Teams' program, earning gold and bronze medals, and later be offered baseball scholarships from Georgia Tech, Louisiana State, North Carolina, and Duke before signing a national letter of intent with national powerhouse Florida State University. He would be named a First-Team High School All-American, and he capped his amateur career by being selected the Gatorade National High School Baseball Player of the Year. In June 2003, Chris became the first-round draft pick of the Kansas City Royals, the No. 5 pick in the nation, and signed with the Royals for a $2.1 million bonus.

Chris was promoted by the Royals to Triple A in the summer of 2007, just one step short of the big leagues ... and yet another opportunity. In many ways, the first really big step in Chris' career was at Fort Myers with Perfect Game, and the folks at Perfect Game continued to provide opportunities throughout Chris' high school years, opportunities which served as a spring-board for him as he pursued his baseball goals. To a great extent, Chris (and many other players) is where he is in his career because of Jerry Ford and the entire staff at Perfect Game.

Today, families can become overwhelmed by the deluge of showcase and other exposure opportunities available. Consequently, players and parents should be proactive in carefully pursuing opportunities through those organizations recognized for their integrity, support, accessibility, results, and innovation. With competition sprouting up at all levels of the industry, Perfect Game USA remains at the forefront, spearheading even more opportunities to help young players achieve their dreams.

Of course, every youngster will realize varying degrees of success as they look to continue their baseball playing experience beyond high school. But when it comes to providing exposure opportunities to many players throughout our nation, Perfect Game USA is second to none.

Wally Lubanski helps parents and players learn about the college baseball recruiting process through his T.E.A.M. Student-Athlete Recruiting Guidance Program, a tutoring service for players and travel teams.

Preface

I became aware of the Perfect Game USA company several years ago while conducting research for a book rating all the youth baseball showcases. That book never came about simply because it quickly became apparent that no other showcase company approached Perfect Game in the quality of events or came close to matching its impact on the pros or college programs. The Cedar Rapids, Iowa–based outfit was decidedly the dominant player, for reasons that will become clear in this book.

Some 2008 statistics provide solid evidence, when Perfect Game set a new record for the seventh consecutive year. Of the 1,504 players drafted into the major leagues, 1,164 were players who had attended Perfect Game events—a total of 77.4 percent. On the college front, 221 players out of the total 277 on the eight rosters of the College World Series were players who had attended Perfect Game events, accounting for nearly 80 percent. The influence is clearly substantial.

The scope of this book is to paint an accurate picture of youth baseball — from the perspective of how the current landscape affects high school players who want to rise to the next level, be that college ball or the pros—along with the history of Perfect Game's impact as the primary agent of change. It's a complex picture, including, but not limited to, the place high school baseball occupies, the impact of select or travel teams and other organizations such as Little League, the rise of steroids and other performance-enhancing drugs, and the role of foreign-born players. The audience for this comprehensive source is historians, researchers and the young player and his family, who need to have an accurate picture and an aid to navigate the sometimes treacherous shoals of youth baseball.

Since baseball showcases in general and Perfect Game in particular are relatively new in a historical sense, my research depended chiefly upon dozens of interviews and personal observation while attending a number of events. The subject is not addressed in another book, and very little in print is dedicated to discussing the relatively recent major changes occasioned by showcases. I also gained valuable insights from the many folks who gather on the High School Baseball Web (www.hsbaseballweb.com), easily the most prominent website for just about anybody involved with youth baseball.

I need to provide a disclaimer. Not only have I been involved in researching Perfect Game for the past four years and counting, I've also been involved with the organization as my son Mike has participated in four Perfect Game showcases as an individual and one tournament with his summer select team. He was also invited to a number of other events sponsored by such companies as Team One, Area Code, Top Guns, TPX, all of which were declined. I felt our experience as participants with the same hopes, dreams and baggage that most parents and players have provided a valuable insight. I've included the positives and the negatives in our family's odyssey through not only the Perfect Game events, but high school ball, select team experiences, and the recruiting milieu.

There is one hole. An NCAA rule handcuffs college coaches from delivering comments on the book's topic: "Institutional athletics department staff members may not endorse, serve as consultants or participate on advisory

Jerry Ford, facing camera, the founder and president of Perfect Game USA, talks with ESPN officials at the 2007 PG WWBA World Championships in Jupiter, Florida.

panels for any recruiting or scouting service involving prospective student-athletes." Half the folks attending showcases to find prospects are college coaches! While I won't report names and colleges and put any coach at risk of noncompliance with Bylaw Article 11.3.2.5, I will pass on my observations as well as many of their comments anonymously.

* * *

One of the motivations for writing this book was delivered by a Fort Wayne, Indiana, high school coach. When I asked his take on showcases, it became evident he was unfamiliar with showcases in general — at least those with national scope — when he answered with a snort: "Showcases! Those are just a guy who owns a stopwatch who wants to make a quick buck!" I was amazed by his attitude and lack of knowledge concerning the biggest force in baseball. What was more amazing was that I discovered he wasn't the only high school coach with this attitude. It is my hope that this book will help inform the many coaches who are simply unaware of the enormous value Perfect Game showcases can be to their young charges in the pursuit of their dreams, as well as to be cognizant of the problems showcases pose.

"You never hear anyone saying their daddies took them to their first basketball game. But you hear it all the time with baseball."
—*Hall-of-Famer Buck O'Neil*

— 1 —

It's Not Your Father's Game Any More: The Rapidly Changing Landscape of Youth Baseball

The beanpole southpaw leaned over and peered in at the catcher to get his sign. Fastball. Low and inside.

The pitcher went into his stretch, checked the runner at first, then lifted his leg and delivered the ball exactly where his battery-mate had called for it and the batter gave a mighty swing at the ninety-three mile an hour heat…

And missed.

"Steee-riiiike three!" screamed Blue in a raspy voice. He added, "This game's over!"— even though no one was listening — the winners were already rushing the mound and their victorious pitcher and the last batter was trudging back to his dugout, head down.

The southpaw's teammates poured to the mound, like ants after sugar, pummeling the flushed lad, burying him under a pile of sweaty, elated bodies, and dimly, at the bottom of the celebrating mass, the pitcher could hear the roar of the home crowd voicing its approval.

Senior year. Last game against their biggest rival. Conference championship on the line. A two-hit, complete-game shutout. Only two baserunners allowed for the entire game. Seventeen strikeouts. He'd even hit a home run and a double and walked once! The only out he'd made at the plate was a towering fly their center fielder had made at the fence.

Dream game in a dream season.

Later, in the locker room, noisy with jubilant players in various stages of undress, taking showers, replaying the game to each other, the highlights, Coach Kirk Begosee walked over to him. Behind the coach stood two adults, one a middle-aged man in a rumpled, off-the-rack suit and a porkpie hat, the other, a young man in his late thirties, clad in a pair of Dockers, wearing a smart alpaca sweater the distinctive orange of the University of Tennessee, and, in case the color wasn't enough, a huge "UT" emblazoned across the front. Oh, yeah — in case that didn't proclaim loudly enough who the man was, he was also wearing a white baseball cap with orange letters that read "Vols" in cursive script.

"Lefty," Coach Begosee said, "that was one of the best-pitched games I've ever had the privilege to witness. What a glorious way to cap off a great season, son!" He turned to include the men behind him. "And, I've got a couple of fellas here who'd like to talk to you. This is John McCloud, one of the top scouts from the Dodger organization, and you may recognize this other gentleman as Coach Rod Delmonico from Tennessee. Mr. McCloud was just driving by and saw the lights on the field and came in to watch the game. He was impressed by your performance tonight and wants to talk to you about Dodger Blue and what they can do for you." Coach Begosee continued. "And Coach Delmonico has read about you in the papers. Even though he's in Tennessee and we're in Indiana, he gets newspapers from all over the country and visits all the kids who get the kind of headlines you've been getting. This is a red-letter day, son!"

*   *   *

Can you spot what's wrong with this story? Well, for starters, it starts out with the wrong kind of language. The first sentence should have said, "Once upon a time." After all, that's the way fairy tales traditionally begin, right?

And, make no mistake — the above is just that — a fairy tale.

There's also no Dodger scout by that name and, although Coach Delmonico did preside over one of the nation's top college baseball programs, he didn't subscribe to newspapers all over the country in hopes of finding talent.

It's doubtful any coach does.

Something like the above fiction may have taken place many years ago — a scenario where the famous college coach and a well-respected and powerful professional scout came to watch a high school player in action — a Brooklyn Dodgers birddog perhaps driving around small towns in hopes of spotting baseball talent — a college coach from two time zones away visiting a player who's earned a stack of press clippings. Maybe... Notice I said the *Brooklyn* Dodgers. Maybe a scenario like that could have happened when the Bums were still in Flatbush.

Today? Not a chance. It's surprising, though, how many people still cling to that romanticized notion of how ballplayers get "discovered."

A high school player today who has aspirations of playing college ball or professional baseball or both simply isn't going to become a blip on the radar of either the pros or colleges this way. That adage that any ballplayer, if good, "will get noticed," just isn't true. Not unless he does something to help himself get noticed beyond playing or even starring for his high school or even summer league team.

There are lots of reasons for this, most of them financial.

College coaches, even the DI big boy "brand names" like Stanford, Texas, Tennessee, Miami, Rice, LSU, Arizona State, and Oregon State, just don't have the money in their recruiting budgets to travel this vast nation to watch high school ballplayers in games. At least not until after they've identified the players they're pretty sure they want. And smaller and less prestigious DI baseball programs and schools in the other classifications— DII, DIII, NAIA, Juco, and academic collegiate leagues such as the Ivy League and Patriot League (neither of which offer athletic scholarships)— have even less in their recruiting coffers.

The fact is, a great many colleges recruit primarily in their geographical area and that's because of not only the lack of money in their budgets, but also the time restraints such scouting would tax on their schedules. And have you priced an airline ticket lately? The cost of even a cheap hotel or motel room? How much bacon and eggs and a cup of bad coffee costs when a waitress serves you instead of eating at home? Car rentals or cab fares or the price of gasoline if you're tooling around in your own ride? Have an inkling of roughly how long it would take to travel around the US of A to eventually settle on the players a coach needs to sign, pro or college? Not to mention getting a look-see at foreign players? Get the picture?

Why, then, do you see players on many college team rosters who are from other parts of the country and other countries?

Simple. These days, colleges scout the top select teams in their area and attend youth baseball showcases and top select team tournaments to find talent easily and relatively inexpensively. What no college coach or pro scout is doing these days is running all over the country or even in their area looking at individuals play in high school games. When scouts and recruiters do show up at a high school contest, it's more to simply confirm what they've already learned about a player through his exposure at a showcase or on his summer select team. They're not there to "discover" anyone. High school baseball has almost become superfluous except for the few nationally prominent "super high school" programs, and even those programs are scouted less than the showcases and select team leagues and tournaments.

It's not only the top DI programs that actively recruit nationally. More than a few junior college programs also have rosters with many out-of-state players, but that's a different situation. Many of those players were unable to qualify academically for four-year schools and look to jucos to get playing time in a competitive arena, and the jucos that are baseball "factories" are fairly well known. Sometimes the goal of the player going to a juco is to beef up a grade point average to qualify for a four-year school and sometimes the aim is just to get noticed by the pros by playing at a prominent juco program.

Expense-wise, all of the above holds true for professional scouts as well. Even the pros have limited budgets for traveling and scouting, not to mention greatly diminished numbers of scouts on their payrolls than in yesteryear. Michael Lewis' book *Moneyball* has hastened a change in the drafting landscape that was already in flux, and one of the results is a decrease in the number of scouts MLB teams employ. Another result is that ballplayers in college are more prized than ever before. That's a part of the landscape we'll examine later.

*   *   *

What has happened to professional baseball organizations and college programs is what has happened in any successful business: a major reduction in personnel and those attendant costs in order to maximize profits and reduce overhead and capital expenditure, just as in any other business. Instead of employing dozens and dozens of scouts, scouring the countryside for talented ballplayers, a relatively new phenomena has emerged that does away with the need for many of those folks.

Baseball showcases.

The new gatekeepers of baseball. The folks who control the pipeline of talent into pro and college ball.

It has all changed the game in profound and complex ways, some of which we're only beginning to realize.

At a top showcase, a college recruiter or a pro scout or agent can see a couple hundred or more of the best high school ballplayers in the region or even the nation at one time. At a top tournament, even more. A great many more. In one such setting, at the Perfect Game World Wooden Bat Championships (WWBA), over 1,000 players from 80 or so of the top national select teams participate and are playing against superior competition. Instead of traveling to LaPorte, Indiana, to see a shortstop, then to Eugene, Oregon, to see a pitcher, and then to Metairie, Louisiana, to look at a power-hitting centerfielder with great wheels, a recruiter or scout only has to travel to one place to see a great number of athletes. This saves the college or the pro team money and time. Plus, the premium showcases have already identified the best players through various means, and the quality showcases are run uniformly, measuring the precise things that college recruiters and pro scouts want to see, such as pop times for catchers, running speed in the 60-yard dash and from home to first, pitching speeds, infield/outfield throwing speeds from all the positions, and other standard skill measurements. The showcases also provide opportunities for scouts and recruiters to see players perform in games against meaningful, quality competition. Another element which can be measured at a good showcase is the young player's "makeup," a baseball term that applies to his personality, among other things. Perfect Game, for example, always has one of their personnel in the dugout with the showcase team and notes are taken on each player's makeup and that information is freely given to any college coach or scout who calls. Makeup is more important than many realize. Both the pros and the colleges place high value on a potential recruit or draft choice's personality. Since a DI only has 11.7 scholarships to divide among an entire team, a cancer in the dugout, no matter how talented he may be, is going to cripple the team. The same holds true for the pros— a player whom the club has invested literally millions of dollars can prove costly indeed if he turns out to be a malignant force.

Four high-level prospects celebrate a teammate's home run at the 2002 Perfect Game WWBA Championship as members of the Perfect Game/Baseball America team. From left, Ryan Sweeney (Iowa, Chicago White Sox second-round pick), Jeff Allison (Massachusetts, Marlins first-round pick), Ian Stewart (California, Rockies first-round pick, and Lastings Milledge (Florida, Mets first-round pick) (courtesy Perfect Game USA).

Participation by the best players in the nation and abroad has increased amazingly over the past few years. The reason? Wally Lubanski, father of first-round draft pick Chris, offers this: "Over time, Perfect Game events have attracted the top players around the country and in each region as well." Here's the key, according to Lubanski. "Talented players draw the coaches and scouts, which then attracts more good players and so forth. Perfect Game continues to move forward with regional showcases, underclassmen events, high profile national opportunities like the Jupiter tournament and the National Showcase, wood and metal bat tournaments, something for nearly every player. Plus, Perfect Game does an absolutely amazing job of planning, organizing, and managing some pretty challenging events, pulling it all off time and time again."

What do you think makes more sense for a recruiter or scout to do? Fly or drive 1,000 miles or even more, rent a room and a car, buy several over-priced meals and spend a full day or two—to see one or two players for which they have received perhaps biased or flawed reports to begin with—or, to spend the same amount of money or even less and see dozens or even hundreds of good players in one place who have been identified by reputable and reliable baseball people as having excellent skills? Not to mention that when the scout gets to the prospect's high school game, the opposition may elect to pitch around him, the net result of the trip being judging how he trots down to first base after receiving his intentional walk.

The players profit the most. According to Lubanski they gain in three ways. His opinion is that, "First, players can get 'prime time' exposure. They get on the radar, which is so critical today for every player. Competition for college baseball roster spots is intense, so players must be diligent in getting out there and being seen by baseball's decision-makers. Perfect Game offers that exposure, and to a degree greater than any other organization.

"Second, Perfect Game provides players with the opportunity to compete against talented players from other parts of the country. How do you stack up against others? Many folks would agree that you improve your own skills by competing with and against other talented players and Perfect Game provides the venues to experience tougher competition.

"Finally, Perfect Game provides players with invaluable feedback; Perfect Game has scouted and evaluated thousands and thousands of players; they've seen the best in baseball. They know what they are looking for and provide evaluations which players can use to further their own development."

Dan Kennedy, who is the Northeast Director of Perfect Game, and who has played a significant role in opening up a section of the country to scouts and college coaches previously neglected, offers this: "No matter what ability level you are you get exposure, especially at events like the Jupiter event, which is the most amazing event in baseball. If you do what you're supposed to do, you will find opportunities for yourself; Perfect Game can put you into any situation you want to be in. Perfect Game has invitation-only events, however, most events are open. Enough events that if you don't do well at a certain event, you can go to a different event and do better."

Quite simply, attending the right showcase is probably the single most important action a young ballplayer can take to get a college scholarship or get drafted into pro ball. Granted, there are other ways to attain a scholarship or be drafted, but no other way can get a ballplayer the same amount of exposure to as many schools and that alone greatly improves not only the range of selection but the opportunities.

And, those "other ways" are fast drying up as more and more young ballplayers learn what the right exposure at the right event can do for their future. The time and energy coaches and scouts spend in the field to find talent has been dramatically reduced in just the past five years and is sure to be reduced even more.

—2—

How the Stage Was Set for the "New" Field of Dreams: A Time of Innocence

The stars and planets of the baseball universe began to come into alignment back in the mid-nineties with a combination of factors. First, the television audience for the Little League World Series, for years of relatively decent size, began to increase dramatically. Part of the reason for the increase in viewers resulted from the jump in professional baseball salaries, spearheaded by Alex Rodriguez's mind-boggling contract of $250 million. That buys a lot of sunflower seeds! While baseball players were hardly paupers before A-Rod's historic contract, his signing catapulted salaries into the area of true wealth. All for hitting or throwing a baseball!

At about the same time, ABC/ESPN, the broadcasters of the Little League World Series, in an attempt to bring Little League baseball to the level of the everyday youth player, began to talk about how the Little Leaguer's pitching speeds "computed" to major league pitching speeds. The networks began to popularize a "formula" for adjusting the actual speed of pitches to account for the closer pitching mound. A Little League pitcher, throwing at the distance of 46 feet and timed at 75 mph, was (they claimed) the equivalent of a major leaguer throwing at the professional distance of 60' 6" at 101 mph.

Suddenly, this single claim had the effect of changing how youth baseball players were viewed by their parents. Fathers would look at their own little Johnny and extrapolate his throwing speed and envision him on the mound at Yankee Stadium. Before this formula was delivered to the viewing public, most parents had a somewhat realistic and a bit more pessimistic view of their sons' chances of ever playing professional baseball. Now, even the dads of ballplayers with average or even modest skills began to harbor unrealistic hopes for their sons. Maybe their pride and joy couldn't be Nolan Ryan but

Little League Pitching Speed vs. Major League Pitching Speed Conversion Chart

Actual Speed	Actual Speed	Actual Time for 46'	Major League Speed	Major League Speed
(mph)	(ft/sec)	(seconds)	(ft/sec)	(mph)
40	58.67	0.784	84.81	57.83
41	60.13	0.765	86.93	59.27
42	61.60	0.747	89.05	60.72
43	63.07	0.729	91.17	62.16
44	64.53	0.713	93.29	63.61
45	66.00	0.697	95.41	65.05
46	67.47	0.682	97.53	66.50
47	68.93	0.667	99.65	67.95
48	70.40	0.653	101.77	69.39
49	71.87	0.640	103.89	70.84
50	73.33	0.627	106.01	72.28
51	74.80	0.615	108.13	73.73
52	76.27	0.603	110.26	75.17
53	77.73	0.592	112.38	76.62
54	79.20	0.581	114.50	78.07
55	80.67	0.570	116.62	79.51
56	82.13	0.560	118.74	80.96
57	83.60	0.550	120.86	82.40
58	85.07	0.541	122.98	83.85
59	86.53	0.532	125.10	85.29
60	88.00	0.523	127.22	86.74
61	89.47	0.514	129.34	88.18
62	90.93	0.506	131.46	89.63
63	92.40	0.498	133.58	91.08
64	93.87	0.490	135.70	92.52
65	95.33	0.483	137.82	93.97
66	96.80	0.475	139.94	95.41
67	98.27	0.468	142.06	96.86
68	99.73	0.461	144.18	98.30
69	101.20	0.455	146.30	99.75
70	102.67	0.448	148.42	101.20

Major league speed is calculated over 66' 6"
using the actual time for 46'.

doesn't Greg Maddux only throw in the mid-eighties? And Jamie Moyer was probably even slower!

*   *   *

A personal story

Years ago, when my own son Mike was twelve and playing for his select team, I was standing behind the fence behind home plate, watching the rival team's pitcher warming up. We played at the "regular" baseball distances, unlike Little League. Bases ninety feet apart, pitching distance 60' 6". Beside me was an elderly gentleman who clutched some type of timing mechanism and who, as it turned out, was the pitcher's grandfather. His grandson threw a couple of warm-up pitches and the man clicked his timer and exclaimed in proud excitement, "Man! That last one was at 58 miles per hour! I wonder how fast that would be at major league speeds?" I looked at him and said, "Fifty-eight miles per hour." He gave me a funny look and then you could see the light dawning behind his eyes. "Oh..." he said, and walked off, head down. It was obvious he was doing one of those "conversion table" estimates in his head, not realizing his grandson had just thrown at the "regular" distance.

I imagine his dream died that day. Particularly since his grandson proceeded to get rocked immediately, giving up seven hits and two walks before his coach mercifully lifted him. Fifty-eight mph was below batting practice speed for Mike's 12U team who regularly faced pitchers who threw in the high-sixties and even low seventies. I have no doubt that this boy was tearing them up in Little League, but in "real" baseball he was decidedly slow.

Confused as this gentleman was about his grandson's throwing velocity, he did represent what thousands of dads and other grandpas were thinking about. That their progeny could make it to the Show. There were now huge sums available for those who could throw fast, and the parents with potential little Herb Scores residing in their households were aware of it. In actuality, the majority of these kids would probably top out closer to former major leaguer Stu Miller's top velocity than Score's. As former St. Louis Cardinals coach Jim Murray once said about Miller, "He's got a fastball you could catch in your teeth. Three pitch speeds: slow, slower, and reverse."

Realistic or not, a great number of the parents watching the Little League World Series and extrapolating their progeny's pitching speeds from the conversion chart provided by Harold Baines and the other announcers mentally projected that their son might, with a "little help," end up in the dugout of the Chicago White Sox or Oregon State University. The "little help" they had in mind included private lessons with former college or professional players, playing on travel or select teams, and, attending showcase venues that promised exposure to the "right" people (i.e., pro scouts and college coaches) that would get their sons on the radar. Web sites, such as former Cincinnati Reds associate scout Bob Howdeshell's High School Baseball Web (www.hsbaseball web.com) emerged as significant sources for anecdotal accounts of how their sons obtained scholarships or got drafted after attending showcases, giving advice as to which showcases to attend, how to find the "right" travel team, what private coaches gave the biggest bang for the buck, and so on.

A national conversation began, fueled by the words of the announcers and commentators at the Little League World Series during practically every game, as they superhyped the "exploits" of the 12-year-olds on the field. The average dad, sitting in his easy chair and watching these games and listening to Baines and company, saw players who didn't look much different than their own progeny being projected as future MLB Hall-of-Famers and began to do their own fantasy projections. What wasn't mentioned by the television commentators was that they were playing the games on fields with extremely short fences where pop flies on a "regular" field became home runs, gushed over by announcers who described the "shots" in Ruthian terms. What wasn't mentioned much was the shortened base paths and shorter distance between the pitcher's mound and home plate. They acknowledged the differences in distances, but dismissed the dimensions as being of much importance. Most of the parents watching didn't pay much attention either — these were fields of the same dimensions that their own kids played on. Many didn't realize that thousands of other kids on select teams played on regulation fields.

The explosion was on. And, showcases such as Perfect Game, Team One, Area Code, TPX, Baseball Factory, Headfirst Academy and all the others became inundated with applications by thousands of hopefuls.

The game was changed profoundly and forever.

— 3 —

The Birth and Early Growth
of Perfect Game USA Showcases

The baseball planets were now in full alignment. With the enormous increases in pro baseball players' contracts and the growth of television audiences for the Little League World Series, the stage was set for showcases such as Perfect Game.

Perfect Game wasn't the first showcase on the scene. That honor fell to a few other companies, notably Team One, the Area Code Games, the East Coast Professional Baseball Showcase, and a handful of others, the majority of the others chiefly local in scope. Team One lays legitimate claim to being the first national showcase. But, Perfect Game was a very early participant, entering the arena with their first showcase in 1993, and has evolved to where it is now without question the biggest and most-respected among most college coaches and professional scouts.

Jerry Ford

The story and history of Perfect Game is overwhelmingly the story of a singular man, Jerry Ford.

Baseball has always been a part of Jerry Ford's life. He grew up in Cedar Rapids, Iowa, and played all sports as a young boy. He was an exceptionally talented athlete. He said that when you turned eight years old, "You signed up through your elementary school and were placed on a baseball team. The teams were sponsored by various businesses, much like Little League." Once Jerry got interested in something, he had to know everything about it — the rules, the history, everything — a focus that continues to this day.

Ford admits he was immature at that age. Part of the reason was he thought he knew more than the people coaching, and, in Jerry's words, "in some cases, that was true."

The pro minor league team in town, the Cedar Rapids Raiders, was affiliated with the Dodgers. In 1954, he spent hours and hours with them, talking to the players and coaches, soaking up baseball knowledge. From that point on, it was pretty much live at the ballpark and talk to the coaches and players. From the time he was ten years old, he was out there practicing with them whenever he was allowed to. All the way through school until he got into Jefferson High School, which had won the Iowa state tournament two years before he got there. When he was a sophomore they had one of the best teams in the state and Jerry thought he should be the starting shortstop and "the coach didn't think so."

They had a practice and an intrasquad game — and the coach told him to go down to the bullpen and warm up Larry McDowell, varsity pitcher. Jerry was a cocky kid and knew it all (his words), and told the coach, "Hey, I'm not out here to warm up McDowell." Coach said, "You're out here to do whatever I tell you to do." Jerry retorted that he was there to play ball. One thing led to another and today he doesn't remember if the coach kicked him off the team or if he quit or if it was a combination, but he was done with high school ball. He then played semipro ball through the rest of high school.

Upon graduation, he went into the Army and once out of the service, began coaching, first Legion and Babe Ruth ball. During his Army days, he married Betty. After being discharged from the Army, he attended Kirkwood Junior College. He finally had to quit college to work to support his family. He began working with the Minnesota Twins as a part-time scout. He had Iowa for his territory and he'd put together a list of the top twenty highschoolers in the state and put on showcases before they even existed, but only for one team (the Twins) in the early seventies.

Ford never knew his biological father, who divorced Ford's mom when Jerry was a couple of months old and disappeared from their lives.

Ford has coached at nearly every amateur level possible. Some of his fondest memories were working with youngsters in the Babe Ruth League and with American Legion teams. In the six years he coached college baseball, his teams compiled a 223–78 record.

All of the teams he has been involved with had several things in common. Ford's teams played intelligent baseball, they played very hard, they had fun, they had class, they ran, and they won. In other words, Ford's teams mirror the man.

If you could pick out one trait that describes best his teams' style of play it would be that they ran other teams to death. In 1991, he was coaching Mount Mercy College, a small NAIA school in Cedar Rapids, Iowa. The '91 team led the nation in stolen bases, setting a national record with 309 thefts in just 52 games. One player, Terry Schneekloth, stole 100 bases, breaking the national small college record for an individual. Just as impressive as the

Some of the more than 400 pro scouts and college recruiters watch the action on Marge Schott Field at the University of Cincinnati during the 2007 PG National, the annual event to which PG invites the top 200 high school seniors.

record was the fact that he was only thrown out nine times in 109 attempts for a 91.7 percent success rate. Schneekloth attributes his success completely to Coach Ford's training. The year before Ford took over the reins, as a junior, Schneekloth had set Mount Mercy's steals' record at 25. Then Ford came on the scene and Schneekloth didn't double his previous year's totals, he *quadrupled* them. He was named to the NAIA All-American first team and also made the All-Academic team, which he'd also been named to the previous year when he was a junior.

The next year's team was without Schneekloth and several other of their best stealers—in all, the team lost 246 stolen bases by graduation. And, they again led the nation in steals while compiling a 42–17 record. In those two seasons combined, Mount Mercy stole over 600 bases in just 111 games. What may be most impressive is the fact that that was accomplished with almost totally different rosters.

Schneekloth was his star, though. Before Ford began coaching him he was already a fast runner, running the 60-yard sprint at 6.7 to 6.8 seconds. After a few months of Ford's coaching he ran a 6.25 sixty at a Busch Stadium tryout for the St. Louis Cardinals scout Tom McCormick.

Remembering his star base stealer, Jerry Ford said that one of the things he wishes is that Schneekloth could have been involved with Perfect Game. "He was just one of the nicest and most talented kids I've ever known," Ford said.

In Ford's view, kids who run have the most fun playing baseball, a different view altogether from that of Billy Beane's Oakland A's. Beane has ordered his manager not to steal and discourages the running game at every turn, but it's pretty hard to argue with the kinds of results Ford obtained from a wide-open running game. Ford no longer conducts the running school with the demands Perfect Game now makes upon his time and it's a shame, because his methods and techniques for training baseball runners are legendary and unique in what they accomplished.

In Ford's own words, the philosophy by which he governs Perfect Game is simple. "Money has very little to do with anything I'm involved in. My biggest reward is seeing kids be successful. We have varying degrees of involvement with these kids. Some we've gotten to know their families well and guided them through the whole process. Some we've even taught how to play. It's just a rewarding experience when they have success. Jason Gerst is an example—he was just a role player on the college teams I coached, but now he's one of the owners of PG. I'm probably proudest of the number of kids I've coached who've gone into coaching themselves—probably over thirty." Players he coached who became coaches include Chris Berry, a former assistant coach at Baylor University, who today is the highly respected pitching coach of the University of Arkansas-Little Rock, and Mark Reardon, the coach at Iowa Western.

Sports agents, pro scouts, college coaches, recruiters and, of course, parents watch play on the field at the University of Cincinnati during the 2007 PG Nationals.

Representative of the respect with which most professional scouts and college coaches hold for Perfect Game is Atlanta Braves director of scouting (the top scout in an organization) Roy Clark, whom my son Mike and I interviewed at the 2007 Perfect Game National Showcase at the University of Cincinnati's Marge Schott Stadium, the site of the event. This is one of the most important events in the Perfect Game annual calendar. Approximately two hundred of the top rising seniors in the country (and beyond — the Dominican Republic was represented, as well as other nations), and between 450 and 550 scouts, agents or advisors, and college coaches and recruiters attend the three-day event. There are more than two scouts in attendance for every player.

Clark, who began his scouting career in 1980 with the Braves, said, "Ever since 1993 when Perfect Game began their events, we've [the Braves] been attending them. They've just progressed to be the best in amateur baseball scouting and that's why we've supported them. In our opinion, with what they do with the wooden bat tournaments, we get the best idea of talent. Selfishly,

they hold two major tournaments in Marietta (Georgia) that I never miss—
I wake up in the morning in my own bed at home and go see the top kids in
the country against the wood bat and against a lot of the better competition,
over and over."

— 4 —

The Professional Scout's View

Former agent Kevin Christman of Diamond Talent, now a San Francisco Giants scout, told my Tristate University student interviewer Cliff Meyer in a November 2007 interview that he'd been attending Perfect Game events "since their beginning." Christman went to one of the first events held in Iowa. "Now," he said, "they are all over the country. The information Perfect Game gathers about players is one of the factors that makes him go, he said. Christman also praised the superb organization of the events, a theme that became familiar in talking to baseball folks. He avowed that Jerry Ford's reputation definitely influenced his decision early on to attend his showcases, a comment echoed by almost everyone interviewed.

When asked to compare Perfect Game to other showcase organizations, Christman didn't hesitate when he said, "Perfect Game is the best in the country.... No, the best in the world." They have contributed in large measure to his success as an agent, he said. "I can be at one geographical location [showcase or tournament] and am able to look at players from other geographical locations. They [Perfect Game] just make it easier. It saves money and time. Also, the players are playing against other high competition and it makes them play more competitive." In his view, the elements Perfect Game excelled at were "their organization, details, knowing how to make adjustments. Their events are their skill. They make the events work like clockwork. They do very well with issues such as rain and fields not being acceptable. They are just really reliable and accessible." I had heard many people echo the same sentiments about Perfect Game's ability to handle unforeseen situations and was able to witness that ability first-hand when I attended the World Wooden Bat Championships (WWBA) in October 2007 in Jupiter, Florida. The day before I arrived, the fields had three solid hours of rain plus many scattered showers earlier. The staff worked round-the-clock and purchased over $20,000 of Diamond-Dry to get the 13 fields at the complex playable and had hired a helicopter to help dry one particularly wet field.

Christman utilizes the showcases as do most other scouts and coaches. He gathers information on and impressions of players while watching their performances and uses that information to build a platform that helps him make the decisions and evaluate players. Most players at the Perfect Game events he attends (the bigger showcases that are by invitation only or the large tournaments in which only the better select teams qualify) are future candidates for the draft, being a year or so away because of their age. However, at some events, the players are draft-eligible. Some of the players he has worked with from Perfect Game events include Chris Lubanski, Adam Jones, and Neil Walker.

For Christman, his most productive event is East Cobb in the summer. "It's a good solid week of baseball," he said. "The WWBA [World Wooden Bat Association] World Championship Tournament in Jupiter, Florida, is also a great event to attend. With somewhere between 80 to 90 teams there are many players to look at. Fort Myers also has a great event to attend that consists of underclassmen."

What does Christman look for when he goes to a showcase? "Athletes. Good physical athletes with good bodies, great running, throwing, strength, and a baseball-savvy mind. Many kids have some of these tools, but not enough. Desire also plays a big role, along with their determination — how they compete and how they stand up to different situations."

He doesn't have a list of players he plans to observe, but does have a follow-up list that consists of players combined from all the previous events he's been to.

To get an idea of what a scout or agent goes through on a typical day at a showcase, Christman gave this itinerary:

"Check in the hotel, get rosters and know what teams the players you want to see are on. Map out your day. You have to plan it so that you get to see the ones you want to see and that they're playing the position that you want to see them play. Observe the players by taking running times, looking at their stance, balance, how they approach the ball. Next, I evaluate the game, study who they are by trying to get to know them. Look into their high school, what college they plan on attending, how they do in class, are they mature, look at their family and relatives, and ask yourself what you're getting yourself into. Will they pay off? Great talent will rise above good talent. Even though there are many good players, there will be some that stick out whether it be in a good or bad way."

Player evaluations are a long-term affair. "We usually spend one to three years evaluating a player," he said. "We want to know who they are, what's the value of bringing in this kid. We look at the risk and reward factor. I bring talent to the team, but then someone has to evaluate it."

He said he also goes to the teachers and other high school faculty of the prospects he has an interest in to get a better understanding of what the young men are like.

Perfect Game events are a godsend to scouts like Christman. "We do a lot of traveling," he said. "We have to go to all ends of the earth to find a good player. You have to put up with bad and dangerous towns, sometimes not getting three meals a day, 4:00 A.M. wake-up calls, fighting to get twenty minutes to work out. You meet young people who could be ambassadors for the game in the future. You have to push and keep the integrity up even if you're tired and hungry. You have to have a lot of pride in your job and believe in what you're doing. You want to achieve the most payoff for the least price. Somewhere along the line you have to put money to the side and find a player that will contribute to the team. They're there for the good of the team."

These are all reasons he views Perfect Game as being crucial to his job. Besides the obvious evaluations of players' tools, the events also provide Christman and others information about a player's makeup as observed by the Perfect Game personnel, who take copious notes about behavior and personalities.

Atlanta Braves national scouting director Roy Clark

Atlanta Braves scouting director Roy Clark, who has been a professional baseball scout with the Braves since 1989, said that ever since Perfect Game began their showcases in 1993 the Braves scouting department has attended their events. My son Mike and I interviewed him at length during the 2007 Perfect Game Nationals held at the University of Cincinnati's Marge Schott Stadium. It was an almost surreal experience, standing as we were just behind the third base stands filled with over 400 (some estimates were over 500 and some went as high as 600) of the most powerful men in baseball—powerful as far as hopeful high school baseball players were concerned. These were the top major league scouts, just about all the coaches from the "name" DI colleges, and the biggest agents and advisors in sports. On the field, in brilliant sunshine and more than 90 percent humidity, were two nines from the 220 players invited by Perfect Game, representing the very best ballplayers in the country (plus players from the Dominican Republic, Canada, and several other countries). Clark demonstrated an amazing ability to provide in-depth answers to our questions while keeping a close eye on the prospects down on the field.

Mike had received one of the valued invitations, but Dad's mix-up on the dates had prevented him from being ready for the event. When he'd received the invite earlier in the summer and I was filling out my calendar, I mistakenly marked July instead of June on it. Not expecting to go until the next month, Mike had just pitched a complete game (victory) for his select

Players wait their turn in the batting cages at the 2006 PG Academic showcase in Fort Myers, Florida.

team, the Indiana Eagles, the previous day, throwing 90-some pitches. There was just no way he would be able to pitch this soon, especially against the caliber of players he'd be facing.

When we'd returned home from the Eagles game the day before, Jerry Ford phoned, asking why we weren't in Cincinnati. After figuring out my error, I decided we'd attend the Nationals anyway, to conduct interviews and take photos.

When asked what set Perfect Game apart from other showcases, Clark said, "As far as amateur baseball scouting was concerned they [Perfect Game] were the best, which is why we support them." Asked to compare Perfect Game with other showcases, he stated, without equivocation, that, "What Perfect Game does, in our opinion, with the wooden bats and with getting the best kids in the country at events like the Nationals and in the two events they do in Marietta [Georgia, at the East Cobb complex], nobody compares. In Marietta, especially — since it's right in our back yard near Atlanta and with those two things— getting the best kids in the country gathered in the best competition and playing with wooden bats and getting to see these kids over and over again, it fits our philosophy which is to see the best kids play with wood, just allows us to do that.

Pro scouts and college recruiters watch future high draft picks and future top DI-to-be prospects at the 2007 PG National at the University of Cincinnati.

One of the perks of playing travel and select ball is that many times the kids are treated to a major league baseball game. Between games during the tournament to qualify for the 2006 SANDLOTT World Series, Indy Bulldogs (they changed their name to the Indiana Eagles the following year) coach Jamie Roudebush took the team to see a Cincinnati Reds game. Shown are teammates and good friends Mike Edgerton, left, and Rob Vollenweider.

"We firmly believe in our summer coverage at Perfect Game events. In fact, none of our free agent scouts across the country have programs like most clubs these days, because we understand we'll see these guys over and over in Marietta and places like here [Perfect Game Nationals], while in the springtime [in their high school seasons] these kids don't get pitched to." Clark sees attending high school games largely as a waste of time. "I went to three games before I saw our first-round pick this year, Jason Heyward, pitched to in his high school games. They just kept issuing him intentional walks. Happens a lot in high school ball with the top prospects. His situation wasn't unusual at all — in fact, it's the norm. And why scouting top prospects at their high school games is many times a crapshoot at best. At Marietta, I could see him play — against excellent competition — for five or six games in a row. And nobody was walking him intentionally.

"It's great to see showcases like this, where we can identify who the very

PG founder and president Jerry Ford, left, chats with David Rawnsley, director of PG scouting, during a break in the action at the 2007 PG WWBA World Championships in Jupiter, Florida.

best players might be across the country, but the two back-to-back Perfect Game events [World Wooden Bat Tournaments] they have in East Cobb in July might, for us, have been even more productive. What happens to those kids [at the East Cobb tournaments] is they play for the trophy ... for the ring. Out here [Perfect Game Nationals], it's great in identifying tools, but at the East Cobb events and at Jupiter [WWBC Championships] we see team chemistry. Even though I love these [Nationals], at the world championships I get to see a kid pitch seven innings rather than just two and with position players and hitters I'll get to see them four, five or six games rather than one like this."

When asked how much Perfect Game has changed scouting, Clark said, "It's changed it tremendously. When I was an area scout I'd have 10–15 camps a year where I was hoping to identify who the top guys were.... And then you'd go to an isolated Legion game or Connie Mack game or whatever.... It isn't that way anymore. Most of the kids go to the showcases now. They go to the East Coast showcase or the Area Codes or to those tournaments at Marietta, and it's huge and it's all evolved from Perfect Game. That's just where we go to find prospects now."

Clark mentioned his criticisms of the Perfect Game experience. "For us [Atlanta Braves] the negative is that any time you have a showcase like this, for the teams that don't work as hard as the Atlanta Braves— they catch up to us. Some teams won't even be represented here because a lot of publications will have a top ten list they get from here [PG Nationals] posted on the Internet, so those are the guys they'll put on their 'hit list' as far as their priority kids to begin looking at."

In an interview, Jerry Ford had mentioned the same concerns: that some organizations and colleges didn't send scouts to events like the Nationals, but just waited for others to post the Perfect Game lists and rankings and made their

Dan Kennedy, director of Perfect Game Northeast, travels in his golf cart at the PG World Championships in Jupiter, Florida, in 2007.

follow-up scouting efforts from those lists. Perfect Game spends large sums of money to conduct their showcases and tournaments and then posts results to their website for free viewing. Other, deeper information is provided only to paying subscribers. This is one of the ways they make their money. However, it is possible for an individual or organization to pay for one subscription to retrieve the broader reports and then use that information to create their own list of players and then they invite those players to their own events, enhancing their reputations as "experts" by giving the impression that their own scouts had identified the invitees.

Most ethical baseball organizations, like the Atlanta Braves, are aware who these people are, and find this behavior as deplorable as does Perfect Game, but there doesn't seem to be much anyone can do about it. To the individual player who's trying to snag a college scholarship or be drafted, the situation is a plus, because they're then exposed to a great many more decision-makers in baseball than just those who actually attend Perfect Game events or subscribe to their information. A fairly good analogy would be to

Carmen Bucci, the founder of Complete Athlete, talks to groups of players during the two days of the 2007 PG Nationals. His company helps top athletes develop the communication and public speaking skills that will be necessary when dealing with agents, advisors, general managers, college coaches and other important people in their paths to the pros or college ranks. His services are sponsored by PG at many of their national events. Bucci, a former player, graduated from Northwestern University's School of Communications, where he was a two-time All-Big Ten shortstop, and was drafted by and played with the San Diego Padres. He later scouted for the Texas Rangers and owned the West Coast Baseball School in Sherman Oaks, California.

the music industry. People download copyrighted music from the Internet, avoiding paying a fair sum for the product they are, in effect, stealing. It's reprehensible, but there's not much that can be done to end the practice.

    Clark values the Perfect Game experience highly. At the 2007 PG Nationals in Cincinnati, which came just a few days after the MLB draft, he told me that, "Even though we just had the draft and we [his scouts] really, really haven't had a whole lot of recovery time, we think it's crucial for us to be here. Not only that, we get to meet the kids and talk to them and this and that and the other, which is extremely valuable. Even though others may not attend and [will] get their lists anyway, there's a tremendous benefit to actually seeing these kids and getting to know them."

An unidentified team takes a much-needed break between games at the 2007 PG WWBA World championships in Jupiter, Florida. More than 80 teams competed, and games took place on 13 fields from dawn to past midnight.

Bob Pincus, the coach of the perennially nationally ranked select team the Central Florida Renegades, says, "Showcases, especially Perfect Game, are all about exposure for kids. If I were to give any advice to a young, talented ballplayer who wants to get noticed by the college and pro scouts, I'd say it's a must that his select team participate in one of the two national showcases in Jupiter, Florida, that Perfect Game USA puts on each year — the World Wooden Bat Championship in the summer and the WWBA in the fall. He'll play before 400–500 [actually, there were in excess of 700 scouts present for the 2007 WWBA] college and pro scouts at those events and nowhere else is that kind of exposure available."

That's the reality today. Like it or not, it's not apt to change. The show-case arena simply works too well in today's competitive environment.

If you wonder why Roy Clark mentions the East Cobb/Marietta Perfect Game events and Bob Pincus talks highly about the Jupiter, Florida, events, Perfect Game holds over a hundred and thirty events each year, and, while

Betty Ford, left, and Dick Vaskey staff the Perfect Game booth at nearly every event.

all are valuable, baseball's decision-makers see different benefits for various of the events and all have their favorites. Also, it might be interesting to note that both Clark and Pincus attend the events at both locales as well as other Perfect Game events across the country.

Does that mean that showcases and tournaments such as Perfect Game conducts represent a win-win situation for everyone in baseball? Not at all.

One group in particular is already at a disadvantage and will continue to be so.

Kids from families with limited incomes. Not just poor people, but people who are considered middle-class. The reason is, it's expensive to play on select teams and the good showcases are pricey. An inner city kid whose family is unable to afford paying the fee for a good select team or the registration fee for a quality showcase may still have a bit of a chance if he plays for a large city school in that there may be a scout or two show up at his games. But, the boy who plays for a small town or rural school and cannot afford to play summer ball for a top select team or pay for a good showcase will most likely remain largely unnoticed or even invisible to college recruiters or pro scouts. It's highly unlikely that any scout or recruiter is going to be at any of his games. As noted earlier, scouts today just don't attend many high school games unless they're there to look at a player they've already identified as having potential.

There are other factors working to make baseball more and more a wealthy kid's sport. The young ballplayer who is likely to be the one developed enough for college or the pros is the one who's not only played for a select team and attended showcases but who has been able to afford pricey lessons that will run from $25 to $100 and more per half hour of instruction.

A Perfect Game Showcase, except for a few events such as the Nationals, at this writing is priced at $549, a cost comparable to most of the other major showcases. Smaller showcases—particularly those local in scope—will usually run about $100. This is just the price to participate. The participant is responsible for travel, lodging, and meal expenses.

A mistake would be in thinking that attending a showcase can be some kind of "magic bullet" because pro scouts and college recruiters there will hand out scholarships or let a player know that he's now on the radar and will be drafted. A showcase is just that—an event in which the player will appear on the radar. A more thorough discussion of what to expect a showcase to accomplish for a young player can be found in Chapter 20.

It's kind of funny. Just when golf—traditionally, a rich man's sport—begins to become a bit more democratic with the advent of programs designed to expose inner city youth to the game—baseball, traditionally "America's pastime" and whose roots come from the cow pastures of farm towns—has become more elitist.

This hasn't happened overnight and there are lots of factors involved.

It's not a coincidence that the landscape in youth baseball began to change about a decade ago with the surge in exposure for the Little League World Series. Egos were instantly engaged and unrealistic dreams began to emerge. At about the same time, well-publicized salaries of MLB players began to skyrocket and the parents of little ballplayers now had goals for their sons they felt reachable. More people have begun to discover the benefits of attending showcases and having their kids play on select or travel teams. More and more, Little League baseball came to be known as rec (recreational) ball, or, more derisively, "daddyball." In one of his books, icon Derek Jeter claimed that if he'd depended on Little League baseball to prepare him for pro baseball, he would never have made it, especially since he lived in a cold northern climate (Kalamazoo, Michigan), and that it was only because he played significantly more games against better competition with his travel team that he was able to master the skills that enabled him to become good enough to be drafted.

Let's look at what happened to get baseball to where it is. What follows is going to be an eye-opener for many.

— 5 —

High School Baseball and
How It Lost Its Luster

The Atlanta Braves' Roy Clark made a telling remark about how the pros consider high school competition when scouting prospects.

"As a matter of fact, we firmly believe in summer coverage [showcases, tournaments, and select/travel teams' games] over all other scouting. We see the best players over and over at Perfect Game events against the best competition in the country, but when it comes springtime, the better players don't get pitched to [in high school ball]."

This is one of the chief reasons Perfect Game's events have become "must-see" baseball for professional scouts and college recruiters and why high school baseball, in many ways, has become almost irrelevant, at least as far as scouting goes.

The truth is, except for a relatively few programs, high school baseball isn't all that good. One of my son Mike's early select team coaches, Rusty Low of the Indy Bandits, told his team of eleven-year-olds that most of them in a few years "wouldn't even want to play on the high school team. The uniforms are usually crappy," he said, "compared to travel team unis, and they don't play very many games compared to travel teams [the Bandits played nearly 120 games that year], and the competition isn't nearly as good as it is in travel ball."

He was prescient. Everything he told these young boys was revealed to be accurate.

When Mike started his first high school game against Fort Wayne South Side High School, he threw a no-hitter for three innings—and then the coach took him out even though he'd only thrown 38 pitches and hadn't broken a sweat. On the way home, I asked Mike how the difference between travel ball and high school felt to him. He said when he faced high school batters, it was easy; he just *expected* to get them out. In travel ball, he said he had to work for outs—the competition was infinitely superior. We still don't have a clue why the coach took him out in that game. The only conclusion that made sense was that he'd planned to keep pitchers in the early games on short pitch counts until their arm strength built up as the season went on, and he must also not have realized Mike had a no-hitter going. If the latter was true, that makes sense, but it doesn't say much about his baseball awareness during games to not be aware his pitcher was in the middle of a no-hitter. I'd just never heard of taking a pitcher out during a no-hitter unless he was hurt, his arm was tired, or some extenuating circumstance like that, but then, this was high school ball and high school ball isn't always logical.

Even when his school — Fort Wayne Snider — won the Indiana state high school championship for large schools, only four or five of the players (and that includes the top three pitchers, who really were studs, along with their catcher) would have made Mike's better travel teams. In fact, the team he's played on the last three years, the Indiana Eagles (formerly the Indy Bulldogs), would have ten-run last year's varsity by the third inning. Their fielding was mediocre, the hitting was weak, and the coaching expertise average at best. Basically, the reason they won the state championship two years ago was that they were blessed with a great catcher and three extraordinary pitchers, who all received DI scholarships. In other words, they had the horses. In Indiana, as in many states, the key to competing for a state championship is having at least one pitching stud. If you have two, it's almost guaranteed you'll win a title. Fort Wayne area team Norwell High School won their class state championship in 2007 with basically one such player, first-round draft pick pitcher Jerrod Parker (ninth overall pick by the Arizona Diamondbacks). The reason is, once you get out of the sectional, all the games are spaced at least three days to a week apart, which means one pitcher can pretty much pitch every game. In truth, one dominating pitcher can win the Indiana state tournament. If they played the tournament as is done in other baseball venues, the best *team* would have a better chance of winning, but under its present structure, it's more accurate to say that the best *pitcher* wins. Even though Snider had three horses on the mound, they only had to go with one of them for most of the tournament. At this level and against the kind of fairly weak competition in the state high schools, it mostly boils down to who has a great pitcher. Against the level of competition, what usually constitutes a great pitcher is a boy who has superior velocity, something that's not so much a result of coaching, but is more a case of genetics.

What happens is when a coach wins a championship like this, unless he goes on to win multiple titles with different squads over a period of years, it's unlikely great coaching had all that much to do with it. Many of these guys tend to believe it's their brilliant game moves that led to victory, when in reality, what has happened is the coach has merely been another example of the "Gerry Faust Syndrome."

Pitcher Mike Edgerton was pressed to play first base at the 2007 Midwest Top Prospects.

Older readers may remember Gerry Faust as the guy Notre Dame hired to be their football coach from 1981 to 1985. Faust came to the Irish from Cincinnati's Moeller High School, where he'd won several state high school championships. His tenure at Notre Dame was a disaster. The eventual take on him was that he'd had success at Moeller simply because he had the best talent in the state. Three-hundred-pound linemen on a high school team usually means your team is going to dominate. Many think that both Notre Dame and Faust himself believed that winning state championships "proved" he was a coaching genius. Actually, even though he created all kinds of complex plays, he could have simply called the same play all game and won. He simply had the best talent in the state and as a rule, on a high school level that's the main factor. Coaching is almost superfluous, unless the coach makes too many boneheaded moves.

When Faust got to Notre Dame, he was suddenly up against other coaches who really did know their X's and O's, and not only that, their squads had as many studs as he did at N.D. The result was he was soon revealed to not be quite the football genius others had imagined he was.

Mike Edgerton, the author's son, a member of the Fort Wayne Snider High School team, pitches against Homestead High School in May 2007.

An excellent example of how little high school coaching matters sometimes is found in the pages of Michael Lewis' football story *The Blind Side.* In his book, Lewis provides the story of the man-child Michael Ober, who was, in effect, a high school version of Lawrence Taylor. His Briarcrest High (Tennessee) coach, Hugh Freeze, was the spiritual descendent of Gerry Faust in that he insisted on drawing up dozens of complicated plays — flea flickers, triple and double reverses, and endless passing plays involving just about everybody on the team who could catch a pass. He ignored Tim Long, his line coach, who all but begged Freeze to just run one play, the gap, in which the quarterback handed the ball to the running back and who then ran at the right butt cheek of, in Briarcrest's case, Ober. The massive left tackle was so large and athletic that he simply moved bodies out of his way like a bulldozer and all the ball carrier had to do was follow behind for significant yardage. Freeze resisted because ... well, if he only ran one play — even a play that worked just about every time — it meant that a superior player was responsible for the wins, not the genius coaching.

The same situation exists in high school baseball, especially in a non-sunshine state like Indiana. The schools that are blessed with a top-notch

The Indiana Eagles select team poses for a picture at the 2007 PG BCS 17U Finals, held at the Red Sox's Terry Park in Fort Myers, Florida, where this photograph was taken. Top row, from left: Dylan Moore, Jake Smith, Patrick Kraft, David Schoch, Mike Edgerton, Zach Binder, Coach Jamie Roudebush. Bottom row, from left: Derrick Mounsey, Andrew Armour, Adam Rusche, Scott Lawley, Jake Fitzgerald, Kyle Crawford. In front: Jack Roudebush, coach's son and bat boy.

pitcher would win most of the time if they simply gave the ball to that pitcher and got out of his way. But then the coaches wouldn't be regarded as brilliant coaches.

High school coaches, of course, don't like to hear this, but it's true in many cases. There are a couple of hundred select teams that could beat the winner of the Little League World Series with relative ease, and even a top high school team could lose to any number of travel teams in their state. This is, I suspect, why so many high school coaches poormouth travel teams and showcases. Once a kid plays on a good select team or participates in a top showcase, or both, he isn't ever again going to look at his high school team with the same regard or respect.

What's happening is that as more and more young ballplayers become aware of select teams and showcases and learn the differences in levels of quality in each, high school programs are going to be more and more devalued and even abandoned except by the boy who either wants a rec ball experience or has to settle for that because of a lack of talent. Soccer and basketball are evolving in much the same manner. Check out the scouts—college and pros— at an AAU basketball tournament and then check to see how many are in attendance at just about any high school game that doesn't have a superstud on the floor.

Like it or not, it's not going to change. That genie has long escaped the bottle. For at least two of the "money" sports (basketball and baseball), players' high school careers are mostly secondary, at best. Something to do to keep in shape until the serious competition begins, i.e., summer travel or select ball, the arena where the pro scouts and college recruiters flock to find their next ballplayers. In the so-called "minor" sports, such as hockey, lacrosse, soccer and a couple of others, the high school season is mostly a time-out period of having fun before the "serious" season with the travel or select teams begin.

High school baseball has become largely viewed by both the pros and the top college programs as largely irrelevant and as a quaint relic.

Some high school coaches accept the reality of the situation, although the majority do not. And, it's hard to blame them. After all, coaching high school ball is what they've lived and trained for all their lives and it's natural to deny the fact that what they provide has been superseded by other avenues for young ballplayers. It's probably also why many high school coaches feel showcases such as Perfect Game and the travel or select team circuit are threats to their future.

A question a high school player might ask himself after reading this book or after experiencing a top-level showcase such as a Perfect Game event: Do I really want to place my baseball future in the hands of a high school coach who thinks that "showcases are just a guy with a stopwatch who wants to make some money"?

In a way, high school coaches are right in viewing showcases and travel ball as the enemy. They're right to do so if they continue to deny the reality of today's market, that it has moved from a high school–centered model to a showcase model. But the high school programs that are aware of this shift can use it to their advantage by realizing they can benefit by their players being exposed to the large numbers of highly skilled players and the superior level of play at these showcases and tournaments. It only makes them better players and better equipped to help take their high school programs to new levels.

Some coaches harbor animosity toward showcases and select teams because they unfortunately have let their own egos get in the way. How else to explain what a parent (who wants to remain anonymous for obvious reasons) related to Blaine Clemmens for his Crack of the Bat column on the Perfect Game website.

The following is their exchange. It's a fairly typical problem.

Subject: Re: CA Underclass Showcase

Blaine,

Thanks for the invitation to the showcase.... My son [pseudonym of Bob] wants to do it [attend the showcase he was invited to] but it may interfere with the high school team tryouts and practices. If there is no conflict he will attend the showcase.

Also, what are your thoughts about a high school coach that condemns these showcases and tells the players that they are wasting their time? Do we look the other way and hope that he doesn't find out, or should they fear his words and wait until summer?

Here is Clemmens' reply:

I can't help you on how to deal with the coach that condemns showcases. All I know is if they were such a bad thing, then hundreds of scouts and college coaches including numerous scouting directors and multiple scouts from nearly every organization would not attend tournaments like the WWBA World Championships in Jupiter and certainly they would not attend in the droves that they do at events like PG National. I can't tell you what to do because I do not have to deal with repercussions ... the truth is that what we do is HIGHLY valued by MLB clubs and DI programs. I am certain that on a daily, weekly, yearly basis, I as only one PG employee get more calls/emails from college coaches, scouts and agents about players than most (maybe not all, but most) high school coaches ... and that is not to even consider how many inquiries PG receives as a company ... why? Because we see more players across the nation than they do and our opinion is based on a BIG spectrum, not a small one.

The parent emailed back:

Blaine,

I totally agree with your answer. Since the time that Bob has gone to numerous major showcases [including the Perfect Game National Showcase] and tournaments he has received letters from 28 different colleges ... some have sent as many as a dozen letters.

I am PG's biggest fan. Here's why I asked you the question in the first place. Many baseball families talk to me because I am a big proponent of the type of exposure PG can provide and have promoted travel ball, in particular the two programs that Bob has played for. These same people called me this week because their kid was told by the high school coach to stop going to showcases. Several were told this yesterday after the coach gave them college letters that were sent to them via the coach that were dated as long as two months ago. Many of these letters were sent by the colleges in early September and early October. The coach said they didn't need to be thinking about college this early until they played for him. The parents thought that this was unfair because they would have liked to have responded before the quiet period. This is why the parents are interested in taking matters into their own hands and wanting to hear from an expert like PG. We are not trying to circumvent the coach. The parents simply want to learn how they can expose their son more, because they were originally told [by the coach that] our high school program was all that their kid needed And now they understand that may not necessarily be true.

...We respect the tradition and the winning attitude at our school. Unlike most schools, our games are an event as far as fan attendance but times have changed a bit. Although high school is still extremely valuable to a player, there are still a lot of coaches that also embrace and understand the value of summer and off-season exposure.

This parent's experience is similar to that of many other parents who have run up against a high school coach who was anti-showcase or travel ball. In fact, it was interesting to read about his friend's experience with the coach who withheld college recruiting letters. This isn't unusual and who knows how many potential college or pro careers were snuffed out before they ever got a chance to happen because of such coaches? My own son Mike had a pitching coach on one of his travel teams who discovered after he'd graduated that his coach had withheld over a hundred such letters from him. This young man, who has asked to remain anonymous, told us that this coach had a history of doing the same to other players in his program. In his senior year he was a talented lefthander, throwing in the low nineties. As the story unfolded, this young man did receive a scholarship, but to a college his coach wanted him to attend, and the player thought it was the only place interested in him since their letter was the only contact the coach had allowed him to receive. The coach had close ties to the school. It's not difficult to figure out what this guy was up to. He wanted to guide the youth to the program of his choice, not the player's choice. I imagine this coach's actions had more than a little bit to do with his ego. It was "evidence" he "helped" his players get college rides.

I've listened to far too many similar stories to believe this is an isolated or infrequent incident. Far too many coaches who want to be viewed as the only source of their players' success in obtaining scholarships.

What can a high school player or his family do if they suspect such shenanigans are going on with their high school coach? Probably not much, unfortunately. College coaches understandably don't want to bypass the coach and correspond directly with the player for fear of alienating that coach, who is still seen as the conduit for influencing the prospect's decision. One solution to alleviate the problem is if college recruiters would also contact the player along with the coach. Some colleges do, but many don't, feeling that if they don't go through the high school coach, the action will be viewed as disrespect by the coach and that would cut off their avenue to the coach for future players. For the most part, the players who are contacted by college coaches are those who play summer ball and are noticed at showcases and summer tournaments.

There is another related problem. It's not exactly a secret that there are high school coaches who will give a biased report to a college coach or pro scout and for a dozen different reasons. An unfairly negative report may be given by some simply because they just don't like the kid or his family. Or, they're into promoting one player over others. A personality issue, resolved by sinking the kid's ship ... or at least not allowing it to set sail. The other side of the coin is the coach who overpraises the player he likes to coaches and recruiters at the expense of the one he doesn't. And then there are cases in which the coach honestly didn't know baseball well enough to accurately judge his player's talents, and promoting an inferior player over a better one in this instance wouldn't be dishonesty but just plain old ignorance. But it happens.

It's odd that while a great many knowledgeable college baseball men and pro scouts readily admit and agree that many high school coaches are deficient in their coaching skills and baseball acumen that they would still rely on that coach's report.

None of this is likely to happen often to the obvious superstar, although it did in the case of Mike's pitching coach and his high school coach. If a kid is throwing cheese, it is unlikely the coach with a personality issue is going to bad-mouth him excessively, at least in assessing his talent. After all, it's crazy to tell LSU pitching coach Terry Rooney that rising senior Joe Bob is a lousy prospect when he's consistently throwing at 94 mph and has touched 97. It's more likely to happen to the player who's a low DI or lower-level prospect.

All this isn't intended to be an indictment of high school coaches en toto. A large number are good men, knowledgeable about baseball, and sincerely interested in helping their kids. However, one of the goals of this book is to present a clear picture of the youth baseball landscape. There *are* more than a few coaches who aren't reliable gauges of talent and have a personal agenda at work. Players and their parents ought to be aware of them.

And high school baseball might be even more meaningless if it wasn't for the fact that all of the state high school associations have rules prohibiting any other baseball activity (meaning travel teams) during the high school season. As it is, most travel and select teams practice every single day they are allowed to until the high school season begins and the minute it's over, they're back out there practicing and playing again. If it wasn't for the current rules, it's safe to say that the majority of select teams would jump at the chance to practice and to also play in games and tournaments for their select team instead of the high school squad, and very quickly, in most states, high school baseball would be extinct, at least in the form it exists in now.

It sounds unlikely that any state would suspend its rules or change them to allow high school players to take part in outside-the-school baseball activities, and it probably is, but stranger things have happened. And with the rise in the strength of the forces in baseball of just the past few years—rising and almost-obscene pro salaries; national television exposure for high school baseball begun by Little League and about to take a leap with situations such as ESPN exploring possibilities with Perfect Game, along with other organizations providing more and more exposure nationally to high schoolers; college baseball becoming more and more a big business because of the increased visibility and stature of the College World Series—is it that great of a stretch to imagine some father suing the state high school athletic organization on behalf of his son, accusing it of "preventing his son from competing in the marketplace" to reserve his athletic services for good ol' James Madison High? In the litigious society we find ourselves in today, perhaps that isn't all that far-fetched.

Look at how the professional leagues have changed their eligibility rules for basketball and football players, allowing them to leave school earlier than ever. Of course, that has swung back and forth. Until a year ago, a high school basketball player could announce for the draft in his senior year and be drafted. Then the NBA enacted a new rule requiring the player to either play at least one year of college ball or reach the age of nineteen. The rules keep changing, mostly based on the benefit to the colleges since all the best players were going into the pros from high school before the rule change. It may be just a matter of time before the high schools begin to do the same.

Baseball is also a sport much like basketball, in that a very young player, albeit in relatively rare instances, can compete successfully in the professional arena. Football's a different story, of course, because of the brute physicality— a teenaged player can be big enough to play in the NFL, but his bones and muscles are not mature enough to withstand the kinds of hits a Bob Sanders can lay on him. There are even exceptions there, as witnessed by Louisville University's Amobi Okoye, who was the tenth pick in the 2007 NFL draft, chosen by the Houston Texans, at the age of nineteen. But this situation is not apt to trigger a stampede of nineteen-year-olds to the NFL even if the rules were to be changed.

The truth is, baseball has young teenagers playing professionally. Not in the United States, but in other countries, notably in the Dominican Republic, Venezuela and other Latin American countries and financed by U.S. professional teams in the guise of "academies" where young talent is identified as early as ten or eleven years of age and then signed to a contract.

— 6 —

The "If You're Good, They'll Find You" Fallacy

"If you're good, they'll find you": This is one of the biggest misconceptions of all in youth baseball and harkens back to a much different climate. The saying would be truer if it were amended to say: "If you're very, very good, they'll find you."

R.W. "Bob" Miller, father of one of the top prospects in the country, gave me his take on that "If you're good..." hoary chestnut. His son is right-handed pitcher and 2008 graduate Quinton Miller, ranked as the 35th best high school player in the country by *Baseball America* and 39th by Perfect Game and an early signee for the University of North Carolina in 2007.

"There aren't too many scouts hitting the local Legion, Connie Mack, Pony, or Babe Ruth games these days," he said. "The old-timers all say, 'If you're good, they will find you.' I don't think the scouts have to look so hard anymore; we have started to make it very easy on recruiters and scouts insomuch that they don't have to find you by beating the bushes any more. Showcase events like the Perfect Game WWBA tournaments bring most of the best players in the country to one place three to four times a year (East Cobb, WWBA Underclass (Fort Myers), WWBA 18U (Jupiter). The sad truth is if you sit back and wait to be discovered you may be waiting for quite a while."

One of the college coaches interviewed (and not quoted by name), is from a part of the country that isn't considered a baseball hotbed. Referring to that drawback, he said, "Perfect Game has changed the way scouting is now looked at. My own experience as a high school player is instructive — when I was a kid, I played in a Perfect Game wooden bat league in high school during the spring and fall and it was about the only way players in my area [Iowa] would get scouted. Before Perfect Game, scouts would miss players because there wasn't enough time to find them all. Sometimes the good players would be playing other sports or they didn't play in a very popular baseball area.

Unidentified college coaches watch players await their turn in the batting cages at the PG 2006 Academic Showcase in Fort Myers, Florida.

Perfect Game does a great job of trying to find all players that should be scouted."

He said that almost all the college coaches he knew had a positive attitude toward Perfect Game when it came to getting information about a player and that while other showcases are valuable, "Perfect Game does the best job of all of them in getting the players seen." When asked if he would personally offer a player a scholarship without having seen him play, based only on the scouting and word of Perfect Game, he didn't hesitate. "Yes," he said. "They just do such a sound job that you can always trust their judgment."

He said the days of college scouts going to regular high school games were over, with two minor exceptions: "1. A scout calls a coach and tells him to go there. 2. A kid sends a coach an email or calls him to come and scout him."

I'll add a third. Sometimes a college coach will attend a high school game, not to really look at a player, but because he knows that from time to time, the particular school is a school that's likely to produce a player who fits his program in the future (perhaps just because it's a school with a large student population and with enough students, a player or two is bound to emerge). He may also want to keep on the good side of the coach in the event he needs him in the future to help recruit a player. The college coach quoted above also said he's like most college coaches in that he just doesn't have the time to go to high school games because he needs to maximize his scouting time and he finds it infinitely more valuable to go to select tournaments, wooden bat leagues and Perfect Game showcases instead. The only "downer" he sees is that it's very expensive for players to be able to go to tournaments and the kids who are financially well off have a better chance to get noticed.

He's also cutting back more on attending high school games because in the past, "I get around a hundred emails from kids each year who all think they're good enough to play DI-A baseball [the level he coaches at], but in reality maybe only one or two could play."

The reason this coach, like many college coaches, gets letters from kids who feel they can play at his level is because they've never been to a showcase or played select ball and all they have to go on to gauge their own talent is from their limited experience playing a high school schedule. One of the benefits of participating in quality showcases or trying out for a bona fide select team is that the player who isn't all that good finds that out quickly.

The aforementioned coach's sentiments about watching high school games to find prospects was echoed by just about all the DI coaches I talked to. Almost to a man, they said about the only time they'd attend a high school contest was to watch a kid they'd already identified and they'd identified the player most of the time through showcases. Several said sometimes they hadn't attended a particular showcase but would download the list of players who'd attended and the information posted. If the prospect happened to play for a high school close enough, and he looked good on the report, the coach sometimes would send an assistant to get a look at him in the flesh. But, virtually none of the DI coaches I spoke with would even consider going to high school games to *find* prospects. And, most of the lower division coaches said the same. A few coaches at very small programs said they were more likely to attend a high school game in their area to discover players because their budgets didn't allow them to attend showcases far away and they weren't likely to be able to attract the top talent from the major showcases. For the most part, these were small DI, DII and DIII coaches and some of the NAIA coaches. Even so, the coaches at smaller programs would, for the most part, only go to a game if they were aware of a particular individual. Not a single coach at any level that I spoke to would just randomly pick out a high school game and attend to find prospects. That method of scouting has virtually vanished.

— 7 —

Dominican and Other
Latin American Players

A large part of baseball's changes are linked to what's happening in the Dominican Republic. When you've got a large number of young boys quitting school at an early age to focus entirely on sharpening their baseball skills in an effort to be eventually signed to a major league baseball contract, you've got a large body of players who are competing at an unfair advantage with U.S. youngsters for the limited spots available in baseball, both on the pro level and in colleges. And, yes, colleges are beginning more and more to award scholarships to foreign-born players, especially a few of the top DI programs and some of the junior colleges that are top baseball schools.

Another element at work is that even though MLB has a rule prohibiting signing a Dominican player until he's 16½, it is well-documented that it isn't unusual for a player to have a birth certificate that's been forged and the player is actually younger or older than the age stated on the document. This further adversely affects the competitive playing field for all players.

The approximate number of Dominican Republic–born players signed to Major League Baseball organizations today is 1,521, of which 1,442 are minor leaguers. At this time, 27 of the major league clubs provide baseball academies in the Dominican Republic. A similar situation exists in Venezuela on a bit smaller scale.

The rules in the Dominican Republic are different from the rules for U.S., Canadian and Puerto Rican players. Each July, any Dominican player who has turned 16½ is eligible to be signed by major league teams. In recent years, 25 to 30 of the top prospects have been signing six-figure deals. Twenty-six percent of all players in the major leagues now come from Latin America.

And it's not an even playing field that players from the United States are competing on. Far from it.

Players from the Dominican Republic and other countries are routinely romanticized by the press. U.S. readers regularly get portraits of poverty-stricken, struggling young boys who use a piece of cardboard for a glove and throw beans to each other to practice batting. Those situations exist, but to imagine that's the normal experience is tremendously misleading. The truth, as it often is, is far afield of what we might imagine. That the great majority of these players come from a background of poverty is accurate. In a country with sixty percent of its population living below the poverty line, that's to be expected. And, yes; often these kids *are* using makeshift gloves and bats and balls created from a sock stuffed with yarn, playing on rock-strewn bare lots.

What hasn't been reported as vigorously as these "rags-to-riches" melodramas is how the successful players arrived in the Show. Part of the journey is many times missing. We get the beginning — the poverty deal — and we get the ending — the arrival in a major league dugout — but we don't as often get as clear or as detailed of a picture of the middle part of that journey.

As radio commentator Paul Harvey might say, "And now, the rest of the story." The story of baseball in the Dominican Republic and to lesser and varying degrees in other countries, is a tale of exploitation, pure and simple, primarily by major league baseball.

Some background, obtained from an article by Dave Zirin in *The Nation* ("How baseball strip-mines the Dominican Republic," November 14, 2005):

All thirty MLB teams scout the Dominican Republic and a great many operate elaborate baseball academies. On the surface, this looks like a great opportunity for youngsters, and major league baseball seems to take great pride in the academies.

The sad fact is, they are getting ballplayers on the cheap. Zirin quotes American sports agent Joe Kehoskie as saying in *Stealing Home*, a PBS documentary, that, "Traditionally, in the Latin market, I would say players sign for about 5 to 10 cents on the dollar compared to their U.S. counterparts. A lot of times kids just quit school at 10, 11, 12, and play baseball full time. It's great for the kids who make it because they become superstars and get millions of dollars in the big leagues. But for every ninety-eight kids out of 100, it results in a kid that is 18, 19, with no education."

Zirin quotes sports anthropologist Allan Klein in *Stealing Home*, who describes the kids waiting each day in front of one of the academies. "If they didn't get signed, it didn't even deter them for a minute; they would be on the road hitchhiking to the next location. And they would eventually find one of those 20-some clubs that would eventually pick them up. And if not, then they might return to amateur baseball."

Roberto Gonzalez Echevarria, a Cuban baseball historian, says in the same documentary that he "takes a dim view of what the major leagues are doing in the Dominican Republic with these so-called baseball academies, where children are being signed at a very early age and not being cared for."

Echevarria, who teaches Spanish and comparative literature at Yale and is the author of *The Pride of Havana: A History of Cuban Baseball,* reports in a *New York Times* article (August 12, 2003) that MLB pays the Dominican Republic $14 million a year for the right to run thirty baseball academies. In Echevarria's words, these academies "serve the role of high school and college players in the United States, except that the only academic component they have is in their name." He also says youth "are signed for a pittance, compared with American prospects." MLB has no comment, and the players' union says it has no role in incidents in other nations.

An article on the subject written by Joe Connor for ESPN.com states that once a Dominican signs his contract he has no more than three years to make it to the next level, the U.S. minor leagues and sometimes far less than that.

Beginning in January, signed Dominicans will play baseball seven days a week, all day long. This is the sixteen-year-old prospect that U.S. players of the same age are in competition with. It's the reason that one out of every seven major leaguers are from the Dominican Republic, a nation with a population roughly the size of New York City and covering roughly the same physical area as South Carolina.

The Dominican Republic, for all practical purposes, has been tranformed into a baseball factory system, supplying products for the major leagues. The rationale is that the relatively few who make it are handsomely compensated and even become millionaires, but what's not talked about much are the great majority who don't make it and are cast aside at the age of 18 or 19, with no education and no skills beyond baseball. And no future. We decry third-world sweatshops where young kids labor all day to provide U.S. consumer cheap jeans and tennis shoes, but really, what's the difference?

Not all baseball management is for what's going on. But what's not to like for these guys? They get a steady supply of superlative ballplayers whose entire lives have been dedicated to one thing only — mastering baseball skills from a young age — and they get them much, much cheaper than they fork out for a U.S.-born player when it comes to signing time and the bonus money offered. Money-wise, it makes absolute sense. I also suspect that at least some of these men aren't totally aware of what's going on in the background and the terrible waste of human lives that is going on in order to produce these fantastic ballplayers. (Although, I'm sure that at least some do know ... and just don't care.) It's also easy to ignore the overall situation and focus on the individual rags-to-riches success stories and pretend theirs is the "usual" story when it's not.

To reiterate: One in every seven major league ballplayers was born in the Dominican Republic and comes to us via a sophisticated factory system. This is a significant part of the landscape.

— 8 —

Steroids, HGH, and Other Performance-Enhancing Substances

There is also the steroid issue with Dominican Republic–born players. Major League Baseball reports that more than half of all pro baseball players who tested positive since the start of the 2005 season to February 2007 — 169 of 289, or 58.5 percent — come from the Dominican Republic, and that includes major and minor leaguers, as well as those who play in the Dominican and Venezuelan summer leagues. Of the 157 players suspended during this time, 37 (about one-quarter) were from the Dominican Republic. The pressure to escape a life of poverty is fierce, indeed, and it may be difficult to blame a 16-year-old kid who's injecting himself in a desperate attempt to escape a bleak future in a country where the annual per-capita income is about $2,500. But blame or not, this is the player the young U.S. ballplayer is competing against. That's a big part of the landscape and is largely ignored by many.

How this influences U.S. players

That this many Dominican players have been caught using steroids isn't lost on minor league players, who see the results sitting next to them on the bench. Fighting for a ticket to the Show and seeing a kid from the Dominican Republic who you know or at least suspect strongly is on steroids about to get called up because of the numbers he's putting up has to at least tempt the U.S. player to do the same and even up the playing field.

The news of steroid abuses over the past decade from all kinds of players from everywhere isn't lost on younger amateur players. How is this going to affect what young, impressionable kids who desperately want to make the

Golf carts with coaches and scouts ring each one of the 13 game fields at the 2007 PG WWBA World Championships in Jupiter, Florida. Even though 160 carts were allotted for coaches and scouts, that wasn't nearly enough, and scouts had to "golf cart-pool" to get around the many fields (courtesy Perfect Game USA).

majors? As of now, there is little overt evidence that high school kids are juicing, but there are some signs.

The reality is that a great many young high school and college players are routinely using such substances as creatine and "The Clear" and "The Cream" and think nothing of it.

I do know that even in a non-baseball state like Indiana a local baseball trainer urged Mike to get on creatine, and in talking to a number of athletes where I teach at DIII Tri-State University, I have discovered that more than a few of them didn't see anything wrong with the drug. Several were using it and had used it in high school as well.

What can be done? Again, as in so many other facets of athletics, we can't turn back time and stuff that genie back into the bottle. Perhaps the only realistic action we can take as a society is to take steps to identify those players using performance-enhancers and provide a suitable punishment for violations. In other words, drug-testing, even at the high school level.

When you consider the stakes at the high-profile events sponsored by

Perfect Game and other showcase companies, drug use is likely to become an issue. None of us are happy about the thought, but it's our responsibility as adults in charge of these young players' lives to do everything we can to insure that the playing field they compete on is as level as we can possibly make it. If that requires drug tests for all the players participating in the PG Nationals or the WWBA World Championships, then let's do it, and just as soon as a reliable test is developed.

— 9 —

The Early Years

The Perfect Game enterprise didn't start out as a showcase company. It began humbly, as a simple indoor facility where local Cedar Rapids, Iowa, kids could go to improve their baseball skills.

Jerry Ford related their early history to me over the phone on Christmas Day, 2006, as he and his wife, Betty, were driving to the World Showcase in Florida. They were passing through Missouri and Betty was driving, leaving Jerry free to handle the phone.

"Along about '92 or '93, my sons Ben and Andy and I came up with the idea of an indoor training facility. Ben was 19 and Andy was 24. In our part of the country, they were both pretty well-known as talented players. In fact, Andy had already set most of the records at Washington High School, which is one of the largest high schools in Iowa — records like home runs, RBIs, batting average — in fact, his records are still standing. Then, Andy went to Indian Hills Junior College and signed with the Cincinnati Reds as a third baseman and was assigned to the Pioneer League, an advanced rookie league, and while there suffered a serious wrist injury which ended his career as hitting was his main strength. Ben went to Indian Hills also, as a pitcher, and was drafted by the New York Yankees. One still playing baseball and the other ending his playing career.

"We'd thrown the idea of a facility around for some time and decided we just wanted a place where young ballplayers could go to get better and get some exposure for the ones who were serious about baseball."

Ignorance was probably a good thing for the project, Jerry says, laughing at the memory. He goes on to recall how it all began to come together and how they came up with key personnel to make their dream a reality. "We didn't know anything about business then and didn't realize our area wasn't a baseball hotbed and wouldn't support something like this. A year or so earlier, I was coaching at Iowa Wesleyan and we had on that team two players who ended up pitching in the major leagues and an outfielder who ended up in Triple A. We were the best baseball school in Iowa then, even though we were a small NAIA school, and Jason Gerst was one of the players on our team — a kind of reserve utility player. But, he was a kid I really liked — a good, honest kid, real coachable, real good personality. I sat down and talked to him about his plans after college and he said he really didn't know what he was going to do, so I told him about this idea the boys and I had and told him that if he'd like to I'd like to give him a go with it and help us start up. Well, one thing led to another, and we ended up talking to Bruce Kimm, an old friend of mine and we talked to Andy again, and it ended up being Jason, Bruce, Brad Stovie [a local youth sports supporter], and me as the owners of Perfect Game. We opened up a facility and it went that way for a year and from that experience, we realized this was something that was going to be impossible to support with just kids from the local area. We decided to open it up to the whole state of Iowa and get the best players from the state and we started a facility."

Stovie, according to Jerry Ford, was "the one guy who believed in us from the very beginning and supported us when things didn't look good. None of this [Perfect Game] would have ever happened without his financial help and confidence. Just as most everyone else involved in Perfect Game, Brad didn't care about making a lot of money. He believed we were doing something worthwhile and important. When people say, 'He's all about the kids,' they're describing Brad Stovie."

Jerry was the one who came up with the name. "The four of us kind of all got together to come up with a name. At the time, there were lots of other facilities out there and one in the East, Grand Slam, that was popular, and I wanted a name that was something like that. So, I came up with Perfect Game. To be honest, the other guys didn't like it at the time, but I thought it would go over big and [laughing] it looks like it may have."

The impetus behind getting into showcases Jerry attributes to Jeff Cornell, who was the scouting bureau staffer for the Midwest, now the cross-checker for the Milwaukee Brewers. "Jeff and I were friends and the scouting bureau came into Iowa in the spring each year to look at players, and the professional rules then were that they could only work out four or five guys at a time. The way they did it was they'd get four or five prospects together at a field and unfortunately, they were not necessarily the best four or five players in the state. As an independent organization, we weren't bound by the rules of major league baseball, and so we could do the same thing they were doing and even more [as far as workouts, drills, etc.] and the advantage we had was we could invite as many players as we wanted to. Jeff's the one who gave me the idea to do showcases, something that would benefit not only the pros, but the kids themselves as a lot more of them would be exposed to scouts."

In those early days, the only other showcases that had gone beyond their regions were Area Code, which had begun a couple of years earlier, and Team One, which had just started. Both did a good job, according to Jerry.

Jason Gerst

Jason Gerst had played for Jerry when Ford coached the baseball team at Iowa Wesleyan College. Gerst had just graduated when Ford began setting up Perfect Game.

His recollection of the early days mirrors Ford's. "I had no idea how difficult things would be to get Perfect Game started and the struggles that it would entail," he told my interviewer, Tri-State University student Mario Ramon. "My very first impression was that we had a quality product and ideas and were doing everything in a first-class manner. To this day, that's still our philosophy — we want to be the best at what we do — and we work harder than anyone else does and always make sure we give the players and coaches who participate the best possible product, no matter what it takes."

When they first began, Gerst's duties involved everything from recruiting, organizing, staffing, and planning, with recruiting being the biggest activity he did. "I started out with the Perfect Game leagues and Midwest events," he said. "Today, all these years later, my job is still all of that, but more in a supervisory role that covers mainly showcases that we do all over the country."

Ford's organizational philosophy has always been toward creating generalists, he told me during one of our talks. People in the organization just lend a hand to whatever needs to be done and just about everybody in the company can do many jobs and they all do. It's not the typical corporate structure at all. I saw an example of that at a couple of the Perfect Game events my son Mike took part in. Right alongside Betty Ford at the entrance to the showcases was Don Walser, the corporation's accountant, greeting scouts, coaches and players as they arrived, handing out programs, things you'd never in a million years see the company accountant do for any other business

Gerst is excited about the future of the company. "From a small Midwestern company, we've grown into truly national enterprise. We're now tying in with major media outlets [ESPN] and with companies such as Rawlings, AFLAC and others. From our tiny start, we've grown into the largest and most accurate scouting report service in the world. Our brand name is basically a household name in the top high school players' homes." He adds, "I was really lucky. I'm really glad I jumped on board coming out of college with Perfect Game, but I just knew Jerry had some exciting ideas that would change the baseball world. And he has. I'm just proud to be a part of that. I

Betty Ford, an unidentified employee and Don Walser staff the gate at the 2007 WWBA World Championship in Jupiter, Florida. They check in coaches, scouts, players and parents and sell merchandise, and they work from dawn to dusk.

just believed in him and what he wanted to do and I was very fortunate he took a chance on a young, eager college graduate with a passion for baseball."

Information for all

According to Jerry, the sharing of information was Perfect Game's "different approach. Our emphasis was placing the players number one. We made our information available to everybody—colleges and pros alike, whether they'd attended the event or not. And we did the majority of our work after the event, compiling the information gleaned at the showcase and then getting it into everybody's hands. We also put on, in my opinion, a better showcase than the others. Our initial emphasis was on getting the info to the pro teams, but that didn't mean we neglected the colleges. We'd send our information to all of MLB as well as to a lot of college coaches. In the beginning, we reported to pro baseball most, and today it's the same to both the pros and colleges."

Perfect Game didn't have the website, but put out a printed scouting report publication which they financed through the players' fees. "We realized from the beginning that for players to get the most out of their time and money, we had to make this information available to the scouts, whether they'd been in attendance at the event or not," Jerry said. "The reason it was initially geared to pro baseball was because of my own background and as time went on it became more and more equal with colleges."

This has allowed Perfect Game to forge far ahead of its competitors. Perfect Game looks first at the players' needs, while most other companies see college coaches and pro scouts as their primary clients.

As noted earlier, the free availability of Perfect Game's player lists presents the risk of an unscrupulous competitor "borrowing" those lists as a source of names to invite to their own events. It's a simple task to type a player's name into the box provided in the PG website and obtain a wealth of information—for free—including complete contact information, running times, throwing speeds, height, weight, complete scouting reports, and a wealth of other information. A complete snapshot, including videos of the player performing.

A boy who participates in a Perfect Game event often begins to receive invitations from many other showcase organizations. He's "suddenly" been "discovered." What the lad doesn't realize is that his name may simply have been culled from Perfect Game's lists and added to another showcase's data base. The communication to him says something to the effect that he's been "recommended as being a ballplayer of talent by a 'recognized' scout."

All of this is known by Perfect Game and is a source of vexation, having their hard work being stolen by others, but they feel there's not much they can do about it. This kind of theft began long ago, with other operators "borrowing" their data and lists from the pages of *Baseball America* when Perfect Game provided their lists of top prospects. Ford takes comfort in the thought that the top pro scouts and college coaches are very aware of the practice and act accordingly by attending and supporting their events more so than any other showcases and tournaments by rivals.

Betty Ford sits at the Perfect Game booth, observing play at Schott Stadium at the University of Cincinnati during the 2007 PG Nationals. A familiar sight at PG events, Betty works tirelessly at dozens of chores.

Radar gun "fudging"

Recently, one major showcase has begun another practice which was reported to me by major league scouts and college coaches who asked me not to use their names for obvious reasons. Over a dozen of these men told me at different times and various events that I attended that the company had begun a regular practice at all their events of "adding" an average of three miles per hour to their attending player's pitching and throwing speeds. It's important to note that the major leagues have been doing this, too. Over and over, I was told by the pros and top college recruiters that one of the best things about Perfect Game was that their reported throwing speeds were "true" and accurate and that they completely trusted the speed given. Such wasn't the case with other showcase events.

It's an obvious ploy designed to achieve two results. One intended result, and perhaps the chief reason it's being done, is to bring joy (and repeat business and great word-of-mouth endorsements) to players and parents, especially parents. What this company is counting on is the player who attends a Perfect Game showcase and is clocked at, say, 82 mph and then goes to theirs and is timed at 85. And, the strategy does work, to some extent, at least among parents. And it's the parents' approval the company is after. It's the parents who foot the expenses of showcases and who talk to other parents and either promote and disparage the particular showcase. Overlooking the fact that it's unethical, the practice at first glance it looks to be a brilliant marketing strategy.

Except, the second intended result, which appeared to work at first, is now backfiring. The other result for the offending company was to have the college coaches and pro scouts offer scholarships to or rate high on their draft boards the players that achieved these amazing pitching speeds. Turns out there are two problems with that strategy. One, baseball men are a skeptical lot as a group. Most adhere to that Missouri philosophy of "Show me." That means they show up at showcases with their own radar guns and stop watches. It doesn't take long to figure out that the speeds that show up on their own guns are a bit different than the speeds the showcase operator is posting ... and it happens to just about every kid. Another problem is that these guys are a friendly bunch, even though they're competitors. They talk to each other. And it didn't take long for the word to get around that this particular company was fudging on reported pitching speeds. The word may not be getting to the general public and to the parent and player who attends that company's events, but it's certainly out there with the decision-makers, and eventually it'll get around to everyone.

This particular company contributes to several national lists that rank high school players, and the word among the baseball men that I spoke to was that they were well aware this outfit routinely rated the kids who'd attended their events a few slots higher than kids who hadn't.

This practice of inflating pitching speeds isn't new. The major leagues have been doing the same thing for a number of years. Most stadiums now flash the speed of their pitcher's throws on the stadium scoreboard, and television broadcasts routinely do the same. However, the *New York Times* and other reporting entities have exposed the fact that pretty much all of these posted speeds are jacked up about three miles per hour consistently. Doing so provides the same wow factor among paying ballpark customers and TV viewers as it does among parents of showcase players.

Richard Sandomir wrote about this practice by MLB for the *New York Times* on October 13, 2006, in an article headed: "Fox, ESPN radar guns average 3 mph difference." He wrote "on Tuesday night during Game 1 of the American League Championship Series, Tigers' reliever Joel Zumaya unleashed two fastballs in the eighth inning that were measured at 103 m.p.h., and a third that was clocked at 102.

"Or maybe he didn't."

Sandomir explained how the network arrived at its reported pitching speeds, which clearly revealed and supported his contention in the article's heading, that the speeds were purposely misleading. ESPN Radio's Jon Miller and Joe Morgan reported the same thing, that the same Zumaya fastballs were coming in at three mph slower than FoxTrax claimed they did. ESPN's readings came from a Jugs gun positioned behind the plate at McAfee Coliseum in Oakland. Miller and Morgan reported that, in fact, *all* pitches by all the pitchers were generally three mph slower than what was being reported. Since then, a number of other investigators have shown this to be true in most parks.

It may seem like a fairly harmless practice to pump up fan excitement for the home team hurler, but there is another negative result. The information from Pitch f/x (the radar system used to get the readings) during the league championship series and World Series is also being routed to Major League Baseball Advanced Media to use in the Enhanced Gameday portion of mlb.com's coverage. Fans, looking at that site, may accept whatever's posted as gospel.

It's also somewhat revealing to see which radar gun is used by showcase companies and by MLB ballparks. It is generally agreed by baseball men that Stalkers are more accurate than Jugs and that Jugs guns are about three mph faster, on average, than Stalkers. The reason for the disparity lies in how each gun picks up the ball. Jim Speciale of the Jugs company says that their guns pick up the ball one foot out of the pitcher's hand and a company salesman says that Stalkers pick up their signal immediately after the ball leaves the pitcher's hand. It's a small thing and not a problem if the person using it is aware of the disparity and how each works and makes adjustments for it. Despite the differences, both are quality instruments. But in the hands of another person who may be a bit unscrupulous, that difference can serve to prove the adage that "figures don't lie, but liars figure."

Both pro scouts and college coaches use both brands and both have loyal followers, but they're also aware of the differences in the way they measure the speed of the ball, and so either gun works just fine. It's only when the "whole story" isn't told that readings are reported in a misleading fashion and the unsuspecting customer (player/player parent) gets a false idea of the actual pitching speed.

And three miles an hour faster is a *big* deal!

Showcase popularity with colleges and pro scouts

First, the majority of high school teams aren't exactly loaded with talent. Even the better teams in a given region, even in a sunshine state, will normally have no more than two or three baseball "studs," and most players with high draft potential or with the ability to play in a premium college program are more often than not the only player of like caliber on their team. Knowing that, opposing teams are most likely to do just what Roy Clark said he experienced when trying to scout Jason Heyward during his high school season. If the player is a hitter, they simply walk him intentionally, or, at the very least, give him nothing much to swing at. A high school star is even more unlikely to see many good pitches in most at-bats. A college recruiter or a pro scout can waste a lot of time by trying to follow around a prospect in a (many times) vain attempt to see him hit, watching team after team intentionally walk the player. College athletic departments and major league baseball scouting offices don't like to waste their employees' time in these kinds of largely futile pursuits. Especially when a sound alternative exists, which it does.

Pitchers sometimes pose a bit different story. Pitching speed is easy to gauge, and there is some value to watching a hurler work a high school game. Some players and parents believe that if their son's team has a great player, one who is going to draw scouts to his games, that their own son is bound to be noticed. That's probably not going to happen. In our own area, last year Norwell High School had an absolute stud on the mound for them — Jerrod Parker, who was throwing in the high nineties. At his first varsity outing, his first pitch was clocked at 99. At his games, there would routinely be from 30 to 50 scouts to watch him. The second the coach relieved him, every one of the coaches left. So, this is probably not a good idea to depend on that method of being discovered.

Instead of the historic model, where scouts drove around the countryside, hoping to get a look at a kid they'd heard good reports of, Perfect Game has reversed the dynamic. Now those same kids travel at their expense (well, usually their parents' expense!) to the showcase site. Untold millions in scouting costs are thereby saved by colleges and professional baseball by this simple change. Not to mention all the other benefits scouts experience, such as seeing much more evenly matched (and superior) competition between the participants.

It's no wonder baseball has embraced Perfect Game, and, to a lesser extent, other similar scouting organizations. The service they provide benefits just about everyone, even the player with marginal skills. Before the rise of events such as the Perfect Game showcases, many young players or their parents held an unrealistic opinion as to their ability. Perhaps the student was a big fish in a small pond or a player who stood out among the weak competition of his particular area. Participating in a Perfect Game event quickly exposes a player who really isn't of the caliber to play DI or professional baseball, thereby saving both him and his family a future rude awakening. On the other side of the coin, many a player who harbored feelings of inadequacy has discovered he does, indeed, have the tools and ability to perform with acknowledged superior ballplayers. A great many players have emerged from a Perfect Game showcase with a newfound confidence in their ability, as they performed admirably with the Upton brothers and the Kobe Clemens of the baseball world. Either way, a player soon discovers accurately just where he stands in baseball.

As do the decision-makers in baseball, the pro scouts and college recruiters.

— 10 —

Financial Woes

For the first six years of Perfect Game's existence, Jerry Ford recalls how close they were to closing their doors. "It wasn't month to month," he says. "It was week to week and many times, day to day. I just wasn't much of a businessman."

In the fall of 1999, six years after beginning the Perfect Game enterprise, they were days away from closing their doors. In walked a savior.

Mark Hanrahan

One of Cedar Rapids' leading businessmen, Mark Hanrahan was aware of Jerry Ford and what he was trying to do with Perfect Game. Hanrahan had made millions with the aviation aftermarket parts company he'd inherited from his father when his dad died in 1985. Before that, he'd earned a BA from Iowa State University in 1974 and then a law degree from Thomas M. Cooley Law School in 1978. When his dad, Donald, passed, he was working for him as a sales associate in the family business, Intertrade.

Under Mark's leadership, Intertrade had grown to 45 employees with revenues of more than $30 million, when, in 1999, he sold the company to Rockwell Collins. Unable to remain a player in the aircraft parts business because of a five-year non-compete agreement with Rockwell, he began volunteering as an assistant high school football coach at Prairie High School to help fill his time. It was also at that time that he became aware of Jerry Ford's financial problems with Perfect Game.

In relating the story of how he came to help Perfect Game, Hanrahan first wanted to make it clear that he "was just the banker." He elaborated. "Jerry Ford is one hundred percent responsible for the success of the company. Jerry understood totally what the scouts were looking for and he was a master at being able to evaluate talent, more so than any person I've ever met. He's a true genius in not only understanding baseball and player's mechan-

ics, but also in how to relay that information to the player himself to improve his
game. He's the best teacher I've ever
known."

About Ford's work ethic, Hanrahan
said, "He worked ungodly hours for next
to nothing—basically, self-imposed slave
labor." His genius, according to Hanrahan,
was providing a platform to help kids
achieve their dreams. He felt that if the kids
were adequately showcased that would
happen.

"Everything Jerry touches in baseball
he turns into a national powerhouse,"
Hanrahan said. "A good example is when
he took a coaching job at Iowa Wesleyan.
There was not much baseball history at the
school—no success in their past. It was
basically a glorified girls' school, and Jerry
turned it into a national powerhouse. They
were the best college team in Iowa when
Jerry coached ... and one of the smallest.
One thing about Jerry is—at 55, I coach
high school football pretty successfully,
and I can see the obvious—but Jerry does

Mark Hanrahan, who saved Perfect Game from bankruptcy and
still serves as a financial advisor
(courtesy Mark Hanrahan).

something I can't do. He could see a kid doing something and say, 'He's moving his shoulder or his feet wrong,' or something like that—things I couldn't
see, and he'd always be right on the money, and as soon as he told the kid
what he was doing, it'd be fixed and you'd see the improvement immediately.
He took my own son Sean whom I'd coached up to then—and he was an all-
star high school player, captain of his team and all of that—and Jerry took
him into the cage and worked with him for half an hour on his swing and
the next day he hit the first home run he'd ever hit at any level. Before that,
I'd been working with him and that didn't work too well!" He laughs. "It's
just that Jerry's instructional ability is unparalleled. Jerry was raised very
poor and he's always worked incredibly hard. When I first met him back in
the early nineties, he'd just started Perfect Game with the three other guys—
Jason, Andy, Tyson—and they all worked incredibly long hours for little
pay—basically slave labor. The gift of Jerry was providing kids an opportunity to show their skills. He was, and still is, incredibly focused on helping
kids. His ability to evaluate kids is just legendary. He sees beyond the mechan-
ical things. He'd see a kid doing something and instantly see the little things

he's doing wrong and is able to show him how to fix them quickly. Jerry is an exceptionally hard-working guy, always stays late, and just figures out things by hard work. For instance, he's a hunt-and-peck typist and for years I was after him to go someplace and take a keyboarding class. But he types faster with his own method he taught himself, so I finally gave up."

Hanrahan suggested to Jerry that they needed to renovate to get more work space and buy computers. "He [Jerry Ford] just didn't have any money," Hanrahan said. "It was clear what he needed to make the business work. He had a great product but he didn't know how to market and promote it."

He laughs. "As God is my witness, the day I walked in, the gas man was right behind me, there to give them notice that he was going to have to turn off the heat because the bill hadn't been paid. We started to work immediately. I was writing checks for $35–$40,000 every couple of weeks. It ended up by me putting four to four hundred fifty thousand into it over the course of the next year. Some of it was payroll, some renovations, working with the guy who owned the building to get a better deal, all kinds of things like that.

"I continue to play a role in the business side," Hanrahan says. "I'm not a baseball man — Jerry's the baseball man — but I help them out with business decisions. I'm back in the airplane parts business after my five-year non-compete clause with Rockwell ran out."

And Perfect Game is financially sound.

— 11 —

Watershed Moments

After escaping financial disaster, things began to come together for the company, and events transpired to allow Perfect Game to become the undisputed king of baseball scouting services that it is today.

One of the early factors that allowed Perfect Game to overtake and pass the competition was when Allan Simpson's national baseball magazine, *Baseball America*, approached Perfect Game about establishing a partnership.

Baseball America

Baseball America, the seminal publication of player development of all levels — the minors, colleges, high schools, youth baseball, the draft — had been the brainchild of the most unlikely of men. Allan Simpson, a Canadian, who had only been involved peripherally in the game of baseball, wasn't even in baseball when he began the publication. He was an accountant near his hometown of Kelowna in British Columbia, about a five-hour drive to the closest minor league city, Spokane, Washington.

His connections to baseball were tenacious and minimal. Eight years prior to the first issue Simpson put out in 1981, he'd spent three summers with the semipro Alaska Goldpanners, also working as the sports editor of the *Fairbanks Daily News-Miner*. He went from breaking into the game with the Goldpanners to being named the original general manager of the Lethbridge Expos in the rookie-level Pioneer League. In reminiscing about those days, Simpson said, "I had the good fortune to watch Dave Winfield break in as a full-time position player in Fairbanks in 1972 and Andre Dawson make his professional debut in Lethbridge three years later."

It was almost an accident that *Baseball America* was even born. As Simpson related in a "look-back" reminiscence published in their 20th anniversary issue in 2001, "The idea for a new all-baseball publication came six months before the first issue was launched. I just decided, more spur of the moment, that I wanted to do something different with my life — even if it meant a calculated gamble." He admits he was more than a little naïve about publishing a magazine. "I mean, here I was, a guy with no publishing background, limited financial resources, few active contacts in baseball and a couple of summers' experience working for and covering a semipro team, trying to launch a national baseball publication out of my house. In Canada, no less."

He continues: "Though I had been a passionate Cincinnati Reds fan for years and followed all levels of the game, that was pretty much the extent of my practical baseball background. And my newspaper background. I had never even taken a journalism course in college. But I wanted to get back into

baseball in the worst way. The hold the game had on me never left." Simpson says with all against him and his dream, there were some positives. "The timing also was right to launch a new baseball publication. As a longtime reader of *The Sporting News*, it was becoming increasingly obvious to me that their coverage no longer had the broad-based appeal it once had. Their coverage of the minor leagues was shrinking. College baseball was a growing force, and yet they continued to ignore it. Their coverage of the baseball draft, an area of great intrigue for me, as inadequate. There was no winter league coverage; no summer league coverage. And yet no one had stepped in to fill the void. So if no one else was going to do it, I thought I would."

Allan Simpson, founder of *Baseball America* and now head of PG Crosschecker, takes a rare break from evaluating talent and adding to the Perfect Game databank at the 2007 PG WWBA World Championships in Jupiter, Florida. In the background is David Rawnsley, head of the PG scouting department. They work closely in scouting players.

It's a decided understatement to say that Simpson succeeded in spite of his inexperience and lack of resources. When he left *Baseball America* to join Perfect Game, his "baby" (originally called the *All-American Baseball News*) was far and away the best publication in its field of coverage. Moved to Durham, North Carolina, in January 1983, when Simpson sold the magazine to Miles Wolff, to whom he'd been introduced by the late Bob Freitas, Simpson remained as the publication's editor until 2006, when he resigned and was hired by Perfect Game to run the National CrossChecker service for them. It was also renamed *Baseball America* when it moved to Durham. As Simpson reported in the 20th anniversary issue: "When the paper moved to Durham ... we had 6,000 subscribers. That number approached 75,000 in the early '90s. We have a staff that numbers 20, with some 50 correspondents all over the globe. We have a book division, separate production and advertising departments, and in-house order-fulfillment capabilities. We've grown to 26 issues annually, while also pumping out annuals such as the *Almanac, Directory, Super Register* and *Prospect Handbook*."

It's helpful to understand the man and the magazine to help understand many of the reasons for Perfect Game's phenomenal growth, for, in many ways they're entwined. Certainly, Simpson's magazine helped decidedly in putting Perfect Game on the baseball map and the reasons both organizations were and are successful is reliant directly upon the characters of both Simpson and Jerry Ford.

The beginning of a relationship

In an interview with Chris Wells, one of my chief researchers, Allan Simpson gave a fascinating, behind-the-scenes account of the factors that eventually led to his resigning from the magazine he'd founded and joining Perfect Game. Here, in its entirety, is that account:

"Obviously, *Baseball America's* focus throughout its existence has been on player development at all levels—the minors, colleges, high schools, youth baseball, the draft, or pretty much anything related to developing players at the grassroots level of the game.

"I first became familiar with Perfect Game in the early to mid–'90s from the pre-draft showcase it would hold in mid–May each year at its home base in Cedar Rapids. The event would attract a lot of draft-type players that basically fell through the cracks or weren't being scouted through conventional means. There were routinely a number of players at the event that weren't playing organized baseball at the time for various reasons—their schools didn't have a high school program, they were ineligible, their college/high school season was complete — that kind of thing. I didn't even know that Perfect Game existed the first two or three years the showcase was held, but I remember being impressed both that this showcase was able to identify

David Rawnsley, left, and Alan Simpson record information on players at the 2007 PG WWBA World Championships in Jupiter, Florida. They will spend nearly every minute bunkered down in the "command center" of the tournament. The command center is two stories above four fields that ring it, and each field is visible through the windows such as is shown on this side.

players with this kind of background and that the talent level was sufficiently strong to attract 50-plus scouts and cross checkers, even scouting directors, at the height of the scouting season [three to four weeks before the draft].

"Once I learned of Perfect Game's existence, I quickly became aware that it was putting on other regional and national showcase events at various locations around the country. It was soon evident that PG was becoming a major player in the blossoming showcase-event business, though it wasn't consistently attracting the high-end talent that some of the other, more established showcase services were getting. The Area Code Games, East Coast Professional Baseball Showcase and Team One were the most recognized showcase events/services in the mid–'90s.

"About this time [the spring of 1998, to be exact] and at my urging, David Rawnsley [now also with Perfect Game as national director of scouting — Rawnsley writes many of the scouting reports on the players] left his job as the assistant scouting director of the Houston Astros to come to work for *Baseball America*. It was my goal for David to significantly upgrade *Baseball America's* coverage in all areas of player development and give us more of an inside-the-industry presence. Among other things, we decided to develop a revenue-producing website model to capitalize on the growing interest in the draft and high school prospects, and we did so successfully for a couple of years with our draft preview coverage. When we realized we were achieving a record number of hits on the *BA* website with our draft coverage alone, David and I decided to branch out and develop our own year-round scouting service, called Prospects Plus, which we owned but was marketed as a *Baseball America* product. P-Plus was designed to provide year-round scouting information to the same people that were attending showcase events— scouts, college recruiters, etc.

"In the spring of 2000, a group that included Catherine Silver and Lee Folger, who had no prior sports publishing experience, bought *Baseball America* from Miles Wolff. It was at that point that I relinquished my remaining ownership share in the company. David also left *Baseball America* at the same time, relinquishing his interest in Prospects Plus, to join Team One, which had recently joined forces with Rivals.com, a successful football and basketball website recruiting/scouting service. With a lot of money apparently at its disposal, it was the grand scheme of Rivals.com/Team One to significantly broaden its baseball coverage at the player development level and effectively squash *Baseball America* in the process. But few of the company's financial projections came close to panning out and rivals.com pretty much abandoned the baseball segment of its operation within a year. It cut its ties with Team One.

"Meanwhile, the very future of Prospects Plus was at stake with David's departure from *Baseball America* and Rivals.com's emergence as a significant competitor. I elected to sell Prospects Plus to the new owners of *Baseball America*, but agreed to oversee its operation. On behalf of the company, I moved quickly in the summer of 2000 to arrange partnerships with the Area Code Games and Perfect Game would provide scouting information from their events to help Prospects Plus remain a small, but viable entity. In return, we would help to promote those companies and offer assistance in other areas.

"It soon became evident that Perfect Game was the better fit of the two for *Baseball America*/Prospects Plus to align with, particularly after it staged the ultra-successful 2000 World Wood Bat Association fall championship in Jupiter, Florida, possibly the best showcase/tournament for high school prospects ever staged to that point. Shortly thereafter, I ended our association with Area Code Games, making PG a sole partner with *BA* in the development of Prospects Plus. With the concurrent demise of rivals.com as a significant baseball competitor, the door was now open for *Baseball America* and Perfect Game to move forward and fully develop Prospects Plus in a true joint-venture arrangement.

"We had both a print and web component to the service initially, but eventually it became exclusively a website scouting service. PG provided all of the relevant scouting information/contact information to the venture, while *BA* handled all website, printing and promotional activities. Though Prospects Plus was a modest financial success over the next several years, Perfect Game's popularity surged and it became the nation's dominant showcase company during its association with *Baseball America*.

"The BA-PG partnership continued until February 2006, when *Baseball America* ownership concurrently decided to end its exclusive partnership with Perfect Game and significantly restructure my duties within the company. Rightly or wrongly, *BA* believed it was in its best interest to not solicit scouting information from only one showcase company. It decided, in addition to PG, it would strike relationships with the other remaining showcase companies—specifically the Area Code Games and what remained of Team One, which had recently been acquired by Baseball Factory."

Jerry Ford's version

Jerry Ford relates his own take on the change. "When *Baseball America* began Prospects Plus, Allan Simpson called me up one day and said, 'Jerry, I don't know how you do it, but you guys are much better at this [ranking players] than we are.' One thing led to another and when Allan was still at *Baseball America* they started Prospects Plus and went to us for info and *Baseball America* provided the marketing.

"We did Prospects Plus and it became very popular with colleges and pro scouts. Then *BA* ran the website and provided the marketing and we provided everything—scouting and ranking the players and providing all the info. This went on for several years very smoothly—it was a good joint venture and we actually made a profit. The first two years or so we did the web site version for them and also did our own scouting report, except it was published in print by *Baseball America*. Then, the magazine's management decided they didn't want to do the print publication any longer and just use the website. I didn't want to do that as I'd been told by many pro scouts that they liked the printed version better as they could fold it up and stick it in their pocket when they went around to showcases. It was just handier for them, they said. That's when we first thought about parting company with *Baseball America*. We still provided the scouting reports and rankings of the players to them. It was a 50–50 operation.

"Then, in 2006, Allan told me that their management was thinking about partnering up with Baseball Factory and I told him we couldn't go along with that. For a long time, we'd talked about Allan working for us when he retired, and when he left *Baseball America*, we grabbed him. He's one of the most respected men in baseball and when he came on board, that's when we started the PGCrossChecker service, which he oversees. *Baseball America* wanted to break off our agreement, but they wanted us to keep contributing to their website in lieu of free advertising. Interestingly enough, at least within three months of starting CrossChecker, we had the scouting and recruiting world all signed up. Within six months we brought in more revenue than we had in our entire time with *Baseball America* and Prospects Plus."

Simpson says, "After creating *Baseball America* from scratch in 1981 and overseeing its evolution into the finest baseball publication of its kind as its founding editor over the next 25 years, I was not prepared to accept *BA*'s decision to significantly scale back my job responsibilities. Fortunately, I had developed a strong relationship with Jerry Ford, PG's president, during the previous five or six years and instead of staying on at *BA* in a diminished capacity, I instead elected to accept Jerry's three-year standing offer to join Perfect Game."

Perfect Game CrossChecker

Simpson continues relating his history with Perfect Game with an account of how he and Perfect Game staff members worked together to form Perfect Game's website scouting service. He said, "With my sudden availability and *BA* electing to end its exclusive arrangement with PG on the same day, the timing was right for PG to end its association with *Baseball America* altogether and launch its own website scouting service. With that, Perfect Game Cross-Checker came into being.

"The ultimate goal of PGCrossChecker is twofold: to produce a revenue site for Perfect Game and to broaden PG's area of coverage from predominantly a high school showcase service to a full-blown player development site with in-depth coverage of college, junior college and high school baseball, along with summer and youth-league baseball, and the draft."

What Simpson didn't say is that even though *Baseball America* is still a viable and respected publication, PGCrossChecker is poised to become the number one amateur baseball scouting site. He's brought to the venture the same energy and level of expertise that enabled him to build his former magazine into the authority it became. While *Baseball America* will most likely continue to be the leading authority on professional baseball at the minor league level, as far as high school, youth, national travel and college baseball goes, CrossChecker is in the driver's seat. Not just dry statistics, CrossChecker is driven by journalistic content written by the very best baseball writers and commentators. It features editorials, articles, the latest player and team rankings, providing subscribers with a true insider's look at the latest information concerning amateur youth baseball.

The AFLAC game

Jerry Ford is extremely proud to be affiliated with the only nationally televised high school game, the annual AFLAC contest, and what they've accomplished, both for charity and for the players involved. In its short history, there is already a lore to the game and dozens of stories, especially about the personalities who have been involved.

Among the celebrities who have participated are Denis Martinez, Stan Musial, Reggie Jackson, Ozzie Smith and Cal Ripken.

"Stan Musial came into town and told a bunch of funny stories and then left," Ford said. "A really gracious, generous guy. The story in baseball circles is that the two rarest things are people who *don't* have an autographed photo of Stan or of Bob Feller!"

For the 2007 AFLAC game, Ford said, they got Reggie Jackson. "During the workouts, he was there and really into it, and even after the game was over he went down on the field to talk to the players.... He was absolutely the best they ever had for the AFLAC game."

AFLAC has sponsored the AFLAC High School All-American Baseball Classic since its inception in 2003. The players are selected by Perfect Game USA, and Sports America, Inc., organizes, manages and markets the event. Proceeds go to aid in the fight against pediatric cancer.

Sports America, Inc., launched the McDonald's High School All-American Basketball Games many years ago. More recently, SAI partnered with Perfect Game to present the AFLAC High School All-American Baseball Classic in 2003. This game has been endorsed by MLB and its Players Association as the country's marquee prep baseball All-American event.

Enter Rawlings

There have been a number of important events in Perfect Game's history that have contributed significantly to their growth. One such moment began to take place in early 2005 when Mike Thompson, vice president of sports marketing of Rawlings Sporting Goods Company, was attending the annual American Baseball Coaches Association show. Thompson was having a conversation with Guerry Baldwin, who runs what is probably the best-known youth baseball organization in the country, East Cobb Baseball, and, as Thompson relates, "We had just finished a conversation and he casually mentioned he was on his way to have lunch with Jerry Ford from Perfect Game in a few minutes, and I said, 'Who's Perfect Game?'"

Baldwin talked about Jerry Ford and his organization and what they were doing in baseball, and Thompson recalls, "that sort of triggered my intrigue button and subsequent conversations led me to ask Baldwin to 'tell me more about them,' and then I recall Guerry said, 'Well, Jerry Ford's son Andy is going to be at the East Cobb complex on such-and-such a day — why don't you fly down?' So I did, and I met with Guerry Baldwin and Andy Ford in a meeting room at the back of the complex at East Cobb, and Andy shared a lot of the makeup of Perfect Game — who they were, what they stood for, what they were trying to accom-

Once Mike Thompson, vice president of marketing for Rawlings, heard about Perfect Game, he knew Rawlings had to become a partner (courtesy Mike Thompson).

plish and so on. That got me to thinking that these were guys we needed to talk to and figure out a way to work with them, and from that conversation it sort of developed into more conversations over a period of time which led me to making a phone call and having a conversation with Jerry.

"After I talked to Jerry on the phone, Jerry, his son Andy, and Tyson Kimm [son of Bruce Kimm] ... and it seems one other fellow who I can't remember right now from Perfect Game, all drove down from Cedar Rapids to my office in St. Louis sometime in the summer of 2006. We all sat down and had a meeting in St. Louis and we all agreed that Rawlings was the crown jewel of baseball and Perfect Game had the ability to run these showcases and tournaments and was hosting the premier players in the country so we knew we just needed to connect the dots.

"After our St. Louis meeting, we had further discussions but we couldn't seem to get anything across the finish line in '06. Then, I made a trip to Cedar Rapids and Jerry kind of walked me through his operation — a lot of the technical components of his operation ... you know, from his data base to the things they were doing with the scouting departments and players and the various associations and premier youth baseball clubs, for example, the East Cobb organization and the NorCal organization — just the very hottest baseball beds around the country — and how they were sending their kids to Jerry's showcases.

"Jerry gave me a snapshot of the various events they hosted which, that, in itself," he said, pausing and chuckling, "I couldn't believe the very amount of tournaments and showcases they were putting on and it just seemed to be overwhelming. They were putting on all these things right across the country—from California right through Arizona, Arkansas, Florida, and various hotbeds up in New England and he went on to show me the kids that were participating in these events and the correlation with those kids that were being drafted.

"The connection between the kids that were participating in their events and the kids that were being drafted was amazing and his ability to identify these players certainly was exactly what we were looking for because ultimately you want to communicate with your end user and ultimately you want your product to be used by the best players."

The two parties continued to talk and explore possibilities of how they could benefit each other. Thompson decided he wanted to see a Perfect Game showcase to get a feel for an event.

"I wanted to see one of their showcases in full swing," he said. "I took a trip back to East Cobb. I went to the 2006 WWBA held in Marietta at the East Cobb complex. The one I went was for the 17U tournament. I'll never forget the experience. Jerry was perched up there in his command center with his microphone and was sort of in the crow's nest where he could see everything going on. I went up there and we sat and talked for 6–7 innings of a ball game and he sat there and showed me what was going on there, pointing out this scout and that scout and this player and that player. For example, he'd say, 'On this field over here are the ABD Bulldogs out of southern California and over here the East Cobb Yankees, and the All-American Prospects out of Port St. Lucie, Florida, are on that field and so forth. The NorCal team is on that field and tomorrow we'll have the Georgia Cougars playing another team.'"

Thompson continues relating his experience and impressions. "I was really intrigued by the talent level, and how big this showcase was, and it just wasn't an everyday 'Saturday-Sunday' tournament; the clubs were coming from all over the country by invitation only and had to qualify to get there and I was just amazed at how talented these kids were. I knew Jerry was onto something.

"After I went to the 2006 WWBA, at that point I knew there was something remarkable here. I took another trip out to Cedar Rapids and Jerry and I just talked — I laid everything on the line and I thought that one thing that was important to Jerry was that he considered Rawlings the cream of the crop in baseball and he understood that by associating Perfect Game with Rawlings that would give him leverage and even more credibility than he already had and we felt the same about them. By Rawlings connecting with Perfect

Game, we knew that would give us the same thing Jerry was looking for — it really *was* a match made in heaven — the 'best of the best' connecting with each other."

I asked Thompson if he was familiar at the time with some of the other showcases and showcase companies, such as Area Code and Team One.

"Yeah," he replied. "I spent 12–13 years in southern California in San Diego [with Rawlings], and you can argue all you want about where the hotbed of youth baseball is in this country, but that area is going to get strong consideration as the best by a lot of people. As a result of working for Rawlings and living and working in that area, I'm very familiar with the Area Code games, the North-South thing that was going on in California, and that was all fine and good, but that was just California. What intrigued me about Jerry was — I don't know if this is a good term or not — but how 'fast' he was, compared to the others. In other words, it wasn't just California — it was Florida, it was Georgia, it was ... it was *all* of the hotbeds and he had *all* of the high level players. When I'd had a chance early on to really dig into his website, I quickly found out that there were kids from all over this country spending a lot of time on that website, looking at statistics, looking at who's who, who's going to be drafted, who's a prospect, who's going to be drafted 1–2–3, and where they stood inside their age group, and y'know, I know his group had just simply burrowed into this thing *much* deeper than anyone else. Jerry doesn't cut any corners and his mindset is not necessarily in running and operating a profitable business—certainly it *is* a profitable business, but in Jerry's mind it's all about running a *baseball* operation. What struck me about Jerry was just his knowledge base. I mean he didn't necessarily have to flip on his computer to name you the kids that were going to be drafted one through twenty in next year's draft. He did that for me — named them when I asked him to — and you know what? This was absolutely incredible. Off the top of his head, he named them and I wrote them down and I checked them in the draft when it happened the next year and he *hit 18 of them right on the head*! This was a year before the draft and he picked 18 out of the top 20!

"What Jerry has done to build a database and the factual information he has at his fingertips that he can provide to the scouting world is just beyond belief. If I was a scout — you almost don't need to go see the kid — just call Jerry."

I told Thompson I'd seen this very same phenomena when I visited the Perfect Game headquarters three years ago and sat in Ford's office. All day long, phone call after phone call and email after email came in, all from coaches and scouts, all wanting to know about this kid or that one ... and Jerry had the information on all of them without having to look them up. Thompson said the same thing happened when he was there on all of his visits. The phone just rings nonstop with coaches and scouts wanting to know about players.

Thompson also noted that there is a wealth of additional information on every player that doesn't appear on the website in the player's report or even on the additional, lengthier reports they also provide, such as for pgcross checker.com, that Ford has at his fingertips in a couple of seconds from their database.

A revealing incident took place while I was sitting in his office one day. The phone rang and it was a famous coach from the SEC. The man called to ask Ford about a high school player from Massachusetts he was interested in. Now, the coach had never seen the boy play in person, and he learned about him from the Perfect Game website and he thought it was a player they might be interested in. The coach had a bit of an emergency, as the slot he had open was for a left-handed pitcher and the kid who'd signed with them had suddenly decided to declare for the draft at the last minute. The coach was scrambling to get his spot filled with a quality replacement.

What happened next was eye opening. Jerry went to the young man's file on his computer and displayed pages and pages of information, stuff that wasn't on the website report and that was incredibly detailed. All of which he relayed to the coach in the next fifteen minutes, along with his personal observations (of which he had quite a few, being, as he always seems to be, familiar with the young man's performance at Perfect Game events). At the end of their conversation, the coach asked Jerry whether he thought the player would fit in at his school, and Jerry told him that he would indeed recommend him — that knowing the player and the school, he felt he'd be an excellent fit. The upshot was that the coach told Ford that he was going to contact the young man and offer him a scholarship on the spot, based entirely on Jerry's recommendation.

This is quite amazing. These coaches have their pick of high school prospects and can (and do) cherry-pick to get the best of the best. It's unheard of for such a coach to tender a ride to a kid without having the coach or a trusted assistant see him play. As it turns out, this incident is not uncommon. Neither Ford or anyone else at Perfect Game even mentions this kind of occurrence but it does happen often.

What's also telling is that, as a parent of a young man who'd participated in Perfect Game events, I knew all about the brief report that was posted for Mike on the website and I also knew about the longer, more detailed report on him on pgcrosschecker.com (a service you pay extra for), but, as I'm sure just about every other player and parent assumes, I wasn't aware any more information on my son was available. Perfect Game doesn't advertise the behind-the-scenes services like this that they regularly provide for players. College coaches and pro scouts are aware that this detailed, additional information is available for just a phone call or email from, but parents and players aren't. Until now.

What's also instructive about Ford's and Perfect Game's attitude and philosophy is that all of that information is always couched in positive terms.

Just about every interviewee for this book laughed and said that everyone in college coaching was aware that all you had to do was pick up the phone and call Jerry and he'd spend half an hour or however long it took to tell you everything you wanted to know about a young man. One coach, who'd just taken a job as the head coach at a Florida school, said it was a shame parents and players didn't know the lengths Jerry went to on their behalf behind the scenes. He said maybe if they knew half of what he did on so many players' behalf, they'd never balk at the cost of a showcase again. I heard similar comments from dozens of college coaches. As one old, crusty college coach told me, "The thing about Jerry is that, one, he knows more about baseball and baseball talent than the majority of folks, and two, and maybe more important, what he says is gold. You can always trust it."

Getting back to Mike Thompson and how Rawlings and Perfect Game hooked up, he said, "From there, we just talked out a deal. I talked about what was important to Rawlings and Jerry talked about what was important for Perfect Game and we put an agreement together..." he pauses. "It's funny we're talking about this. I just met with Jerry at the winter meetings [the winter 2007 MLB meetings which had just ended a week before our interview], and we decided it'd be a good thing to get together in January (2008) and just recap everything we did in '07 and just kind of look at successes and how to build upon this thing and make it stronger. I'll tell you — here's an example of just one of the great things Jerry came up with the year before in our recap meeting. He said, 'Mike, let's put together a preseason All-American team and we'll call it the Rawlings Preseason All-American Team' and we did the first one this year ['07]."

Thompson related how the team was chosen. "Basically, it's Jerry and his team of Perfect Game 'wizards' that really pick the team. Jerry and I will confer back and forth on it, and Jerry will call up a week after he gives us the list and say, 'We need to tweak this a little bit.' What was really startling about the whole thing — and I don't have the exact data in front of me — is guess what happened to the players that were selected as the preseason All-Americans at the end of that journey after the season was over? Those were the kids that were drafted in the first round. It was scary how close they were to Jerry's picks!"

When asked how Rawlings' partnership with Perfect Game worked these days, Thompson said, "While we have a contractual arrangement with various deal points on it, it's really more of a 'I'll call Jerry and say, 'Hey, Jerry, what do you think about this? I've got an idea.' And, even though we have a deal point contract, if it's something that's good for baseball or good for the kids, we'll just do it. A good example of how we work together is Jerry called me once and said, 'Hey, Mike, we're involved in the AFLAC All-American game — do you want to be involved?' And I said, 'In what way?' And he said, 'How about donating the baseballs for the game?' And I said, 'Yeah, that makes perfect sense — yeah, we'll do that — it's the high school All-American game, why wouldn't we?' Really, the way we're involved, I guess — the importance from our point of view is I think Jerry's main asset — his gold nugget — is his data base. Some 66,000 kids pass through Perfect Game's events each year and the statistical data base he has and the ability he has to reach those kids, be it sending them a piece of literature or congratulating them on certain feats or just staying in touch from a Rawlings' point of view. That in itself — just the ability to communicate with the kid is where the value of Perfect Game is for Rawlings. There are a lot of players in this game and it helps to substantiate and validate your brand in conjunction with those people [Perfect Game] who are doing the same thing.

"One of the merits of Perfect Game," he continues, "is that they're the 'best of the best' — they *are* the gold standard. And, on the flip side of that — not speaking for Jerry, but I think that's sort of how he views Rawlings in the context of the baseball equipment field — and so, when you can put two people who are at the top of their game inside their industry ... then one plus one equals three."

Thompson was shocked the first time he traveled to Cedar Rapids to visit Perfect Game's headquarters. "It always amazed me how this little sleepy community called Cedar Rapids, Iowa, has everything working against it being the epicenter of baseball, which is what it's become, due to Perfect Game. For all the hotbeds of baseball — be it south Florida, or all of Florida, or the southern states, California for sure, Arizona — I mean, you'd think that if baseball was to plant a seed that was going to become the center of where things important to the game would take place, it would be in one of *those* locations. How Jerry has managed to build this thing from Cedar Rapids, Iowa, is, to me probably the most remarkable thing of all, but it really speaks even more to what Perfect Game is all about. I mean, when he started out, he had to get on planes and fly and drive all over the universe and just had to go to a lot of places. A lot of work!"

Perfect Game is a family, Thompson said, and Rawlings is delighted to be part of that family. The key to their successful relationship, Thompson said, is that, "we both just understand each other. There's business people and there's baseball people, and I think that's a key connection between Rawlings and Perfect Game that, although we're running a business, our business is baseball, and we 'get' what they're doing and vice versa."

There is no way Rawlings could keep up or attend all of Perfect Game's events, Thompson said, but we don't have to. "Jerry is very good at identifying where we should be. You know, Jerry will say, 'There's this underclass event in Fort Myer that I think you should be at.' Or, 'You ought to come to the Jupiter event — this is big. We're hosting the East Cobb event — this is important.' Jerry has a couple of proprietary events on the board that we'll be engaged in. He's just very good at identifying the events where we should be at and that way, rather than spread ourselves thin, we can pool our resources and make sure we make a bigger splash at the larger events.

"The staff we send to Perfect Game events are comprised of two different kinds of personnel. There's a core group inside our building [corporate headquarters in St. Louis] that are product/brand management folks on the marketing side that we send, and then we have a research and development group that we send around the country. The R&D staff design the products and at the Perfect Game events they have the opportunity to interview and interact with the players and coaches and find out exactly what the high-level kids are looking for. The product people will do the same thing. It's typically a core group of inside people that we send to events. The irony of this is that three years ago when you mentioned Perfect Game to our people, you'd have to explain it over and over what they stood for. Now, when you say 'Perfect Game' there isn't anyone inside our organization who doesn't know what we're talking about."

Thompson relates a story that illustrates this well. "In the early stages of putting this partnership together, I'd just returned to St. Louis after my final meeting with Jerry in our efforts to put this thing together, and I was talking to one of the guys in our office — I think it was our president — and he said, 'Well, where were you [that past weekend]?' I said, 'You'll never believe this, but I had dinner with Jerry and Betty Ford,' and he said, 'The president of the United States?' and I laughed, and said, 'No, the president of Perfect Game in Iowa.'"

Thompson related another very telling incident that happened. He told about a college coach (unidentified, due to the NCAA rule), who had dropped in to the Rawlings headquarters as coaches often do, and during their conversation, Thompson asked him, "Coach, beyond dropping in to visit us, are you here to look at any kids in St. Louis? I know it's early and some of these kids are just getting geared up for baseball." The coach said, "You know what? I'm really not. My whole recruiting thing has shifted. I really can send someone on my staff to one of these Perfect Game showcases and see a lot of talent. I don't even need to go to any [unidentified well-known youth baseball national organization] games any more. I haven't been to any [unidentified national youth baseball organization] games in two years. That's really sad to say that, but it's true. The players just aren't there [like they used to be]. I can see so much more talent at one of the Perfect Game showcases."

Rawlings provided an important element to Perfect Game events that had been missing. As Thompson tells it, "One of the things Jerry would have a difficulty with, is when the pro scouts came to see a pitcher — they want to evaluate the kid and make a judgment on where the kid would land at a major league level if he could land at a major league level, and it's kind of hard to do that when the kid is throwing a high-seam type of baseball [the kind used universally throughout high school, travel/select team, and all of youth baseball], and once the kid makes the transition into the pros and has to throw the pro ball, which is a flat-seam ball, he may well turn out to be a vastly different pitcher."

So, Thompson says, "We developed a kind of baseball for Jerry that emulates the major league ball — the major league seam — and now the pitcher can be scouted by any scout across the country at a Perfect Game event, throwing a major league seam, and if he's throwing a flat-seam ball and it's breaking 6–7 inches, that means a hell of a lot more than if he's throwing a high-seam ball."

The different ball alone puts Perfect Game miles ahead of the competition insomuch as the pros can get a much truer take on pitchers than they can from hurlers throwing the high-seam high school ball. Just as a great many players see their baseball careers end when they have to begin hitting with wood bats instead of aluminum, so do a lot of pitchers see their dreams die when they can't get the same break on their curve or slider with the flat-seam pro ball that they did with the raised-seam ball. Before Rawlings provided the flat-seam ball for Perfect Game events, pro scouts didn't know if the lights-out pitcher they were watching could maintain the same movement when he began throwing the pro-type ball. Now they can see immediately if he has the real goods or not.

Another advantage Rawlings brings to their partnership with Perfect Game was mentioned by Thompson. "We manufacture equipment for major and minor leaguers to collegiate and high school players all the way down to a kid's first glove and bat," he said. "One of the advantages we provide Jerry and the Perfect Game organization is that we're a *baseball* company, meaning we manufacture the whole gamut of products for baseball, which means the consumer can do 'one-stop shopping.' From the uniforms, to bats and balls, catcher's gear — you name it — clear across the board. Unlike other manufacturers who may be an apparel company or supply catcher's equipment or make bats — Rawlings does it all.

Guerry Baldwin and East Cobb (Georgia) baseball

East Cobb baseball has long been recognized as one of the premier youth baseball organizations in the country and probably *the* premier program in most baseball insider's eyes.

Ford talks about how they teamed up. "East Cobb has always been one of the top programs as far as winning goes— they've won all the major national championships there are ever since they came into existence. I talked to them at one time about sending their teams to our events and they said their kids didn't need our tournaments or showcases as they got so much exposure at their own events. We understood that and still scouted their players and then one year, some things happened that made Guerry Baldwin, their head, see the value in Perfect Game and he said, 'We're getting involved right now,' and the next thing we know, their kids are going to all of our tournaments and showcases.

"At first, they wanted us to do something at their complex and we hedged around awhile.... They just had more talent than anyone else. Another part is the intimidation factor in East Cobb. Guerry is very ... don't know the exact word ... hard to deal with. He's not an ump's best friend.... But we did do it because the circumstances were right. It just made sense to do a big tourney in East Cobb. We did and it ended up being the biggest scouting event in the nation in the summer. We just began it three-four years ago and it became a monster....

"Over the past few years we've been doing the tournament in East Cobb, I've got to know Guerry and the rest of the people there, and I found out there isn't anybody in the entire country that's more interested in the kids than Guerry Baldwin. Lots of guys will say that about themselves, but in his case he really is."

Partnership with ESPN

In 2007, Perfect Game announced a working relationship with ESPN. Details of the partnership are being worked on and will be released at a later time, but Perfect Game is now recognized by ESPN as the "leading authority in youth baseball" in the words of ESPN's press release:

"This association with ESPN will help us continue our mission of promoting baseball at all levels," said Perfect Game President Jerry Ford. "Amateur baseball will benefit greatly, which is a major goal of both ESPN and Perfect Game. ESPN and Perfect Game share a desire to help young people fall in love with the game of baseball. Creating baseball fans is just as important as creating baseball players at the grass roots level. We are very honored and excited to team up with ESPN," Ford said. "There is no one who has a bigger impact on baseball or sports in general."

— 12 —

The Parts of the Perfect Game Organization

Perfect Game has evolved into an extremely complex organization, offering a great many services and benefits to young ballplayers. Besides the partnerships and various elements already discussed — PGCrossChecker, Rawlings, the AFLAC game, the Perfect Game Foundation, the emerging ESPN partnership — there are a number of other parts to the whole that are important in gaining a more complete picture of just how much of the youth baseball landscape Perfect Game occupies.

WWBA: Perfect Game established the World Wood Bat Association to govern the many highest level PG tournaments, including the October event, which is the no. 1 scouting attraction in all of baseball. The championship games of the Marietta, Georgia, tournaments have been televised by Fox Sports South.

Skillshow: Tom Koerick, Sr., and his son, Tom, Jr., both run this company, which was an early partner with Perfect Game. They're home-based in Radnor, Pennsylvania, and I've seen them at their booth at every PG event I've attended.

The firm videotapes all the participants at Perfect Game events, posting clips of their skills on the PG website. They've pioneered the recruiting video business and have an extensive file on thousands of baseball players. (They also are involved in other sports.) For a reasonable fee, they offer PG participants a top-notch recruiting program, Athletic Career Tracking System (ACT), which is available for free to college recruiters and pro scouts. Recently, they are working out details with PG's BaseballWebTV to provide the video for their product as well. They can be accessed from the Perfect Game website or from their own webpage at www.skillshow.com. The Koericks, two of the nicest guys you'll ever meet and consummate professionals, have helped thousands of young ballplayers achieve their dreams.

Scouts gather to watch a game at the BCS 17U Championships in Fort Myers, Florida, in 2006.

PGCrossChecker.com: The scouting wing of Perfect Game is www.pg crosschecker.com and is directed by Allan Simpson. Simpson was the founder of *Baseball America* (the publication) and was the editor there for 25 years before leaving and joining Perfect Game. There are over 25,000 players who have individual scouting files in pgcrosschecker.com. Perfect Game maintains several amateur baseball websites including www.perfectgameusa.com, www.worldwoodbat.com, www.baseballwebtv.com and www.pgnational academy.com. Perfect Game also maintains the world's largest database of amateur prospects.

BCS — Metal Bat Division: Perfect Game's Metal Bat division operates under rules similar to those that govern the WWBA. This division was created at the request of college coaches who would prefer to see prospects swing aluminum bats because that's what they use in competition.

Leagues: Perfect Game has run scout leagues in its home state of Iowa for over ten years. Every single player from Iowa drafted by MLB clubs in the past ten years has played in the PG Leagues. PG has begun Scout Leagues in California and in Florida with more to come in other states.

Latin America: In the past five years Perfect Game has helped a large number of Latin players who have signed with major league organizations.

Parents and coaches watch as their sons take batting practice at the Boston Red Sox Terry Field complex in Fort Myers, Florida, during the 2007 PG Academic Showcase. To be invited to an academic showcase, players must exhibit top grades and SAT or ACT scores.

AFLAC Classic: Perfect Game is the official selection partner for the nationally televised AFLAC Classic. All players are selected by Perfect Game. Thirteen of these AFLAC All Americans were selected in the first round of the 2007 draft.

Instruction and Training: Baseball players from all over the country come to train at Perfect Game's indoor facilities in Cedar Rapids, Iowa. Their training center is open to the general public as well as to the serious competitor. The facility has pitching machine cages, indoor dirt mounds, two full size hitting areas, fast pitch softball machines and pitching areas, and a weight training room complete with universal gym equipment and free weights. Perfect Game's staff is made up of former professional and MLB players, college players, and coaches. Their baseball professionals are available for hitting and pitching instruction at competitive rates, and memberships are available.

PG Foundation: Perfect Game has established a non-profit foundation to help promote baseball and help deserving young people. It has a special interest in helping promote interest within inner city kids.

PG Academy: Perfect Game runs a full-service baseball training academy in Florida.

PG Sports Medicine: Perfect Game operates a division that specializes in injury prevention and training.

Academic showcase: This is one of the best ideas from Perfect Game. A number of colleges and universities have higher academic standards than others and before this event (and others, such as the Headfirst Baseball Academy, which is also a quality event) coaches at Ivy League and other top academic schools wasted time going to events where many of the athletes, while great ballplayers, didn't have the SATs, ACTs or grades to be accepted at their schools. What Perfect Game did was create annual showcases open only to ballplayers who not only had superior skills and abilities, but also possessed the rigorous academic requirements and the SAT and ACT score ranges necessary for admission to their institutions. Coaches attending this showcase would know that virtually every player on the field was a qualifier.

— 13 —

The Cultural Impact
of the New Era:
A New Philosophy

The story of Perfect Game USA wouldn't be complete if the story just below the surface of a simmering battle between two opposing forces in baseball wasn't included. An ongoing philosophical argument between the entrenched old guard and the new mindset created by statistician Bill James, the founder of sabermetrics, and carried to fruition by general manager Billy Beane and his Oakland Athletics, as reported in Michael Lewis's *Moneyball*.

Instead of the time-honored baseball tradition of "projecting" a young baseball player's potential—from such factors as a player's swing or pitching mechanics or the way he looks in a uniform—Beane pays more attention to what a player has actually accomplished during his college career. It is rare that Oakland drafts high school players. The reasons are several. First, that's a luxury the A's feel they can't afford.

What Beane realizes is that high school players play against competition that is all over the charts in terms of measurable quality. For instance, a team that won the state high school championship in Indiana may not be much better than a team in Kissimmee, Florida, which finished in the middle of their conference and didn't even make it to their state playoffs. Throw in a host of other factors such as the disparity in the way high school contests are scored. For instance, one team may employ a parent or other relative of one of the players as scorekeeper and the error that boy just made at shortstop may well be recorded as a base hit, while on another team with an unbiased scorekeeper, the same play may easily have been listed as the error it really was. College is where teams like Oakland look for players to draft, simply because the competition becomes much more quantifiable because of the improved level and consistency of the competition.

There has always been an argument in baseball about which is more important — raw ability and skill or observable results — and it is an argument that will probably never be settled. Beane's method of judging talent is derisively referred to as "performance scouting" by the old guard, who instead look at bodies and mechanics and project in their minds what they think a player *can* do in the future.

Also, it isn't that the Oakland A's are against drafting studs and don't understand their value. If they had the same budget as, say, the Yankees, there isn't much doubt that they would apply a more traditional value to their prospects.

The "old school," which represents the vast majority of baseball men — although the Billy Beane model has gained and continues to gain new proponents (see Theo Epstein of the Boston Red Sox, for example) — looks more to the traditional methods of measuring skill. This is the camp Perfect Game falls in. Projecting a player's future based on his mechanics, body type, potential genetic influences, performance against superior competition, and character, primarily.

If you're a Billy Beane advocate, that isn't altogether a negative thing. Even the Oakland Athletics look at many of the same qualities in a player. The difference is, they place a lot more value on accomplishments, primarily college accomplishments. They've built their philosophy around groundbreaking statistician Bill James' theory that "the strike zone is the heart of the game." There are other differences between the two schools. Beane's scouts also place a premium on a player's ability to get on base in whatever manner he can — walks, primarily — while the format of a Perfect Game showcase doesn't allow walks. Once a batter has three balls, the pitcher must throw only fastballs until the at-bat is concluded by either a strikeout, hit, or ground- or fly-out.

Base running speed is also another talent that Perfect Game and most of the baseball establishment prize highly. Beane scarcely looks at that; indeed, he's even gone so far as to prohibit his manager from having players steal bases. Steals, when they go right, lead to runs. When they go wrong, they lead to outs. And outs, to Billy Beane, are the most precious resource the offense has.

Shades of Earl Weaver

Beane's philosophy of baseball offensive tactics is akin to former Baltimore Orioles skipper Earl Weaver, who also eschewed stolen bases, hit-and-run plays, and sacrifice bunts, in favor of his players getting on base any way they could. Weaver highly prized walks — and counting on a big blow — an extra-base hit or home run — to bring the runners home. As Weaver says in his book, *Weaver on Strategy*, "On offense, your most precious possessions are your 27 outs." And, "If you play for one run, that's all you'll get." Like Weaver, Beane drafts for role players more than "studs," believing in and using his bench extensively.

Weaver's offensive philosophy was often as misunderstood in his managing days as is Beane's today. Many assumed Weaver only played for the "three-run homer," neglecting the necessity that to have a three-run homer, the team needs two runners on base. Two of the three runs that Weaver played for came from walks and base hits, and both Beane and Weaver firmly believe that a walk truly is "as good as a hit," for *all* of their hitters. Both men go against the collective wisdom of the establishment, and it's hard to argue with both men's results.

A walk is as good as a hit ... or is it?

Walks are considered with at least slight derision in Little League. The weak hitter isn't dumb — he knows the coach doesn't have faith in his batting ability and just wants him to get on base any way he can — with a walk or even getting hit by a pitch — and he knows it's an insult. That attitude travels upwards as well (or, more likely, it traveled "downward" years ago), to (from) the major leagues and to the "stud" baseball schools, the gatekeepers of those venues graduating from and being influenced in their own youth by this attitude. That players are aware of the prejudice against walks is evidenced in the popular (and true) saying Dominican Republic hopefuls have, that, "You don't get off the island by walking."

For all Perfect Game's strengths, perhaps their chief weakness is that they don't give a prospect a chance to show his ability to get on base via a walk — to, in effect, demonstrate he knows and understands the strike zone. In their defense, a showcase doesn't really allow for the exhibition of this skill. The "customer," i.e., the pro scout and college coach, don't want to see players take pitches and work a pitcher. They want to see swings.

It's really an unavoidable weakness of the showcase format. Besides, if a coach or scout is interested in seeing if a batter knows the strike zone, he can determine that at a later time by attending the player's high school or select team games and observe how he handles an at-bat.

This isn't a criticism of Perfect Game's (and other showcases') failure to measure a player's knowledge of the strike zone as would be evidenced by allowing walks during the games. This would be largely impractical for them to do so, considering the constraints a showcase venue has and what most scouts want to see. But is intended solely to point out that while showcases are valuable for the player, the scout and the college coach, they do have some inherent limitations.

I asked Jerry Ford what his relationship with Billy Beane was—after all, Ford is acquainted with nearly everybody in pro baseball and universally respected—and his reply was "None." He went on to add, after a brief hesitation, "I doubt if he even knows who I am." That perhaps speaks volumes about the two camps.

One of the problems with the scouting mindset in general is that the ability to get on base via a walk is ignored or certainly not highly prized as a player asset by a great many baseball men. This most likely goes back to that Little League attitude toward weak hitters, that the only way such a kid can get on base is to draw a walk or get hit by the ball. It isn't a skill that many coaches at any level spend much time teaching. As John T. Reed points out in his excellent self-published book, *Youth Baseball Coaching*, if a ballplayer hasn't learned the strike zone by the age of nine or ten, it's highly unlikely he ever will. "His habits are too ingrained by that age." (Reed self-published his book because, he says, he didn't want to have to censor or restrict his advice to the establishment, as he knew he would have had to had he published in the mainstream press.) In other words, he was well aware of the bias from the majority of baseball people against some of the principles he wanted to espouse in his book. Self-publishing, he felt, allowed him to be completely honest. Like Beane, Reed adheres to a philosophy outside baseball's mainstream. What also unites them is that they're both proven winners and usually with lesser talent than their competition. *Athletic* talent, that is.

Reed provides a great tool in his book that can help a young player learn the strike zone. He draws a square within a square, labeling the inner square "hitter's pitches" and the surrounding square "pitcher's pitches." Both squares together represent the strike zone. There are four of these "double squares on a line and the hitter's name begins each line." Each of the double squares represents an at-bat during a game. He suggests that a parent grade each player's at-bat. The location of each pitch is marked on the square and the result also marked. Before there are two strikes on an individual, the batter is instructed to swing only at hitter's pitches and graded accordingly. Once he has two strikes, he has the entire strike zone—hitter's and pitcher's pitches—to swing at. With two strikes he has to protect the plate. The results of his swing aren't the important thing. If he strikes out or makes an out in any other way, but does so only swinging at hitter's pitches for the first two strikes, he receives a good grade. If he hits a home run, but hits it off a pitch (before he has two strikes on him) that's a pitcher's pitch, he gets a poor grade. It's a tool to teach a young boy the proper strike zone. Reed's contention, one I happen to agree with, is that the time to teach a hitter the proper strike zone must take place is before he reaches the age of nine or ten.

I have some first-hand experience with Reed's system of teaching the strike zone to youngsters. When my son Mike was eleven, we both decided we were done with the politics of Little League and he went to play in the Fort Wayne Wallen League, an American Amateur Baseball Congress (AABC) league. They had the local reputation of being made up of players and parents who felt the same way we did—namely, being fed up with all the abuses of "daddyball." Mike and I quickly discovered a refreshing environment, absent of much of what was wrong with Little League. Another wonderful thing was that they used the same dimensions as "real" baseball and used most of the same rules. None of that, "the runner has to wait until the pitch has crossed home plate to leave first base" nonsense. The distances between bases and the pitching distances were the same as high school, college, and the pros. Real baseball!

(As an aside, it was because of many of the excesses Mike and I had been subject to and witness of in Little League that we co-wrote a spoof on daddyball that same summer, titled *Surviving Little League*. Two years later, it came out from Taylor Publishing, and we were guests on over forty radio shows from all over the country. As recently as this past summer (2007) we were guests on MSNBC to respond to a Little League issue. We'd like to express our gratitude to Little League for furnishing us with truly terrific material.)

I coached a team in the league and it was one of the most enjoyable years of my life, baseball-wise, even though our team was 1–14 at the time of our last regular-season game. We won our final game, and because of the way we won it, I was selected as the all-star coach for our division, over other coaches who had much better records. Wallen was a league run by parents who didn't just give lip service to the goal of teaching kids how to play baseball properly ahead of wins; they backed up their words with their actions.

Here's what happened. I introduced several concepts that were new to my players. Fortunately, even though these were revolutionary ideas, the kids (and their parents) bought into it. The first and biggest change I introduced was to explain that we were going to have each player work primarily on learning the strike zone. I felt at this age it was more important to work on their futures in baseball than it was in winning games. This is like what Little League managers *tell* their kids at the start of each year, but which rarely ever comes true. About the time the team is zero and six, the manager reverts to whatever it takes to win, including playing his best players most of the time. That was a concept I threw out immediately. Little League requires each player to play a minimum of one inning in the field and have at least one at-bat. Wallen's rules were much better in that regard: Each player had to be in for at least two innings. But, I told our team, "Everybody is going to play the same amount of innings on this squad." I mean, these were twelve-year-old players in a rec league, not the New York Yankees chasing a pennant. Also, I was reasonably certain the Chicago Cubs weren't sending secret scouts to see how I was doing, in the event they suddenly needed a savvy skipper.

The author, left, and his son Mike prepare for one of two back-to-back appearances on MSNBC News. Adjusting Mike's earpiece is David F. "Cowboy" Durham, a cameraman and producer for NBC in the Chicago studio. MSNBC invited us to speak about youth baseball, and Mike stole the show (photograph by Mary Edgerton).

From Day One, we began teaching the strike zone, using Reed's "box within a box" tool. A parent would fill out each player's at-bat and we'd assign a grade. It didn't much matter what kind of result the boy had. All we were interested in was if he learned only to swing at pitches in the "inner" box, the hitter's pitches, before he got two strikes. For example, if he hit a triple with no strikes and hit it from a place outside both boxes (a decided ball), he got at most, a C. If he struck out, but from taking two pitcher's pitches and then missing a hitter's pitch, he received a B+.

What we were mostly interested in was teaching the kids the proper strike zone and that if they learned the zone they'd do much better at the plate in later years.

One other thing I tried to get the team to do as a whole was to bat left-handed. This is perhaps one of the biggest areas of misconception in all of baseball — that batting is a "handed" skill. Throwing is, but hitting isn't. I'd like to say that I learned this on my own, but that wouldn't be true. I have to tip my cap again to John Reed, who taught me that. Like just about everybody else, I just assumed that if you were right-handed, you naturally hit right-handed, and, if left-handed, you should hit from the left side. After all, just about everybody in baseball (I thought) accepted that as baseball gospel.

I was dead wrong. I was in the same boat as Reed when he discovered that handedness doesn't play a role in hitting whatsoever. As he admits in his book, "I and my two oldest sons bat right-handed. My youngest son, however, bats left-handed. The reason is I got over being stupid by the time he started playing baseball."

Swinging a bat is an athletic skill exactly the same as swinging an ax to fell a tree. Think about it. It doesn't matter which side you swing from, does it? It feels "right" from both sides. The reason batting from the left side of the plate feels awkward to players who've always batted right is just because of that — they've made thousands of swings from the right side of the plate and very few from the left, therefore it now feels awkward. But, if you take a kid who's never batted before and is just beginning, *both sides feel equally awkward*. As far as what "feels" right to an older player, that depends solely on what side he's always batted from and not at all from the fact that he's left- or right-handed.

Here's a little-known and interesting fact: A predominant number of coach's kids bat left-handed. Look around your own area and see if you don't see the same phenomena. It's because a lot of coaches already know that there are a great many more advantages to batting left than right and that it isn't a handed skill. Or, they may actually believe it is a handed skill, but they have their sons and daughters bat left anyway, believing that if they begin early enough they can "teach" their kids to overcome the "unnatural" side — that the benefits of batting left over right are worth it. They're only half right. They're right that there are far more advantages batting left, but wrong when they think they're teaching their kids to "overcome" a physically biased stance.

So if coach's sons bat left-handed at a far greater percentage than other kids, why don't they let other parents in on their "secret"? I imagine you can figure the answer to that out.

The Lefty's Advantages

According to John T. Reed in his book *Youth Baseball Coaching,* there are ten advantages to batting left. They are:

• The batter is closer to first base.

• The batter finishes his swing facing first base, rather than with his back to first, as does a right-handed hitter.

• A left-handed batter "sees" the pitch better if facing a right-handed pitcher.

• Home plate is not an obstacle to left-handed batters.

• Left-handed hitters can drag bunt whereas righties can't.

• Left-handed is better for pull hitters for three reasons:

1. Most second-basemen and many first-sackers are right-handed, which makes it harder for them to throw to second to start a double-play.

2. With only one runner at first, most first basemen play close to the bag to hold the runner, leaving a hole for the left-handed pull hitter to take advantage of.

3. A runner on first is more likely to advance two bases on a hit to right field than to left because the right-fielder has a longer throw to third.

• Opposite-handed hitters have an easier time hitting breaking balls.

• Left-handed batters block the catcher's line of sight to the first base runner.

• Left-handed batters are in the way of a right-handed catcher's throwing arm.

• Most batters are right-eye dominant and therefore hit better left-handed.

Anyway, I was unable to get the kids and their parents to buy into batting left as a team, and it was probably an impractical goal to begin with, seeing as how the kids were already 11 and had their batting habits ingrained solidly. However, as Reed claims, even if a boy is 11 or 12 and has always batted right, he can still master hitting from the left side of the plate. What he has to do is begin hitting off the tee, left-handed. Reed allows that after 10,000 swings from the left side, the player will then be as good from the left as from the right and will only get better and better from that point. Also—and this is a huge selling point for batting left if you believe it (I do)—a player batting left, Reed says, will always progress to at least one level higher in baseball than he would batting right.

We improve game-by-game

My Wallen team lost games and lost some more. But three things were encouraging. One, the margins of our losses were getting closer and closer.

Two, the hits we got were solid hits — not fluke hits that were really errors by the opposing defense. And three — and most important of all — we ended each game with more and more walks. Toward the end, we were losing most games by a run or two at most.

And then the final game came, against the top team in our division, a team composed of the best athletes in the league. All free-swingers. If they didn't swing at everything close to the strike zone all throughout their time at-bat their coach screamed at them. "If it's close, swing!" was a familiar refrain from his dugout, which proved he didn't have the faintest idea of the difference between hitter's pitches and pitcher's pitches and how to work the count.

It wasn't even close. We won 15–3. (Oh, yeah, Wallen didn't have that insidious ten-run rule either.) On three hits. Two smash doubles, both line drives to the fence that good fielding kept to doubles, and one single that should have been a double or even a triple but the boy was held to a single by a monster throw on the line from deep in right field to second.

But we collected fourteen walks. *Fourteen walks.*

It was simply an amazing testimonial to what we'd been teaching all season. Every single kid on the team except three got at least one walk. (Remember — I used every kid on the team for equal innings.) Just about every time one of our guys got a hit the bases were juiced. And the other team just kept on walking runners in.

Earl Weaver ball. Billy Beane ball. John Reed ball.

Our only regret was the season was ending, not starting. We'd finally "gotten it," as a team. Not a single player got less than a B for his at-bats. Most received A's. Every single kid came away from that season with a sound knowledge of the strike zone.

We received another piece of good fortune as well. We drew a good plate umpire. He was so unlike many of the umpires Mike and I had experienced in Little League. He actually knew the strike zone and enforced it. Also, he didn't try to speed the game up by widening the zone as had been our experience in Little League (especially near the end of games). I wish I could recall his name to give him his due props.

We carried our success over to the all-star game. Not as well as our regular team did — I only had three of our kids on that team — but even so most of the other kids on the squad tried to emulate what our three boys were doing once we explained how it would make them better hitters. The all-star game turned out to be the longest game in Wallen history. It started at seven and ended just after midnight. The opposing team was doubtlessly the more talented team. We just wore out their pitchers with our at-bats. Before it was over, they'd used nine pitchers. We'd used four. Just about all of their pitchers were better than ours, save for two. But they weren't used to facing batters who really knew the strike zone and were as disciplined as ours, even the kids who hadn't been on our team. But kids are pretty smart. When they saw how we'd won our last game, they figured out it was a pretty good system — after all, most of the kids chosen for the all-star team came from the squad we'd beaten. And, if they weren't convinced at the beginning of the game, when they came back to the bench after whiffing on pitches clearly not hitter's pitches and having to hear our kids deriding their efforts, they straightened up quickly and got with the program.

This is the "flaw" in much of scouting — not measuring the ability of a player to get on base. It is what Billy Beane means when he tells his scouting department that, "We're not selling jeans." He, Reed and others feel that drafting a player because he "looks like a ballplayer" is not a smart move.

Reed addresses the topic of walks brilliantly. He claims that walks are even more important than hits, for what seem to me, at least, logical reasons. For one thing, when a batter works the pitcher for a walk, in general, that pitcher has thrown more pitches on average than he would if the batter had struck out, grounded, flied out, or even gotten a hit or been hit by a pitch. That means the pitcher won't go as deep into the game as he would if the batters he faced were all swinging.

This was the "secret" of the New York Yankees during Manager Joe Torre's early years with the Bronx Bombers, in my opinion. He insisted his players be patient in each at-bat, and the result was, besides more walks — ergo, more baserunners to knock in — the opposing hurler's allowable pitch count was many times reached by the fifth or sixth inning. That meant that the opposing manager had to bring in his middle relief guy far earlier than he'd wanted to. And middle relief is the weak spot in most team's rosters. Just about all major league teams and top DI teams have lights-out ninth-inning closers, but very few have top middle relievers. If you go back to those early years of Torre's reign, you'll see a great many games in which the Yankees were tied or behind until the fifth or sixth inning and then ended up winning, many times by sizeable scores. Even at the end of his career with the Yankees, Torre's hitters were more patient at the plate than many teams, but they seemed to have lost the iron discipline they'd shown in earlier years. They were not nearly as patient as they had been earlier in his regime. And the results prove it.

I've included this because it points out perhaps one weakness in showcases. They don't provide an opportunity for the player who knows, understands, and utilizes the strike zone to his advantage to draw walks or work the pitcher for "his" pitch. Many of the young men selected for showcases in general are superior athletes and most selected for Perfect Game showcases are able to hit even "mistakes" out of the yard, but when they get to the Show and face equally superior pitchers who aren't required to throw only fastballs after a three-ball count, their weaknesses begin to get exposed.

With all of this noted, in truth, most of the baseball establishment, including Perfect Game, doesn't appear on the surface to be all that concerned about Billy Beane, his scouting and playing philosophies. But I suspect they are, even if they don't talk about it. Careers have been affected already. In Toronto, Rogers Communication bought the Blue Jays and appointed Paul Godfrey, the former mayor of the city, as CEO. Stuck with a limited budget to build a contender, he interviewed several baseball men for the job of general manager. All had the same pitch for the job — "Give me enough money and I can build a champion." Not what Godfrey was looking for in a helmsman. He found his guy in J.P. Ricciardi, who was employed as the director of player development for the Oakland Athletics. A Billy Beane disciple, who laid out a plan for Godfrey to build a contender with limited funds, ala the Billy Beane method of evaluating players. One of the first things Ricciardi did upon assuming the job was to fire twenty-five of the Blue Jays' scouts.

A few other clubs began moving toward the Beane philosophy. The Los Angeles Dodgers hired Oakland's Paul DePodesta with an aim of improving their ball club with Beane's principles. DePodesta had been all set to take over the Oakland G.M. job when Billy Beane first accepted an offer to run the Boston Red Sox. Then, Beane reneged, opting to remain with the A's. DePodesta's reign with the Dodgers lasted two years and ended up with him being fired. Perhaps it was just a bad fit and perhaps he wasn't given long enough to complete the job. He ended up being hired by Sandy Alderson, CEO for the San Diego Padres, as a special assistant for baseball operations. Alderson was the former Oakland G.M. who had hired Beane in 1990 as an advance scout, and, like Beane, was a man who believed in much the same way of evaluating players.

When the Red Sox couldn't get Beane, owner John Henry did the next best thing; he went after and hired Theo Epstein, a man who viewed Beane as his role model. Epstein seems to have the best of all possible worlds — the opportunity to use Beane's techniques but with a much more significant budget. This perhaps, makes traditional baseball men more nervous about their future than the small-market success of Billy Beane. After all, at one time the Oakland A's success could be viewed mostly as an aberration, but the more clubs that adopt the Oakland philosophy, the more the old way of evaluating prospects is being challenged.

It's instructive that Epstein allowed Johnny Damon to go to the hated New York Yankees rather than matching their bid. I suspect it may be due to the fact that Epstein was fully aware that the A's had done the same thing years before in letting Damon leave for the Red Sox simply because in their method of evaluation he wasn't as good a leadoff hitter as most fans and traditional baseball men rated the centerfielder. To replace him, Epstein applied the same philosophy as Beane.

To date, only a handful of clubs operate under the principles of Beane, but as they continue to succeed, there will probably be more. Until (and if) that happens, more than likely the game will remain as "business as usual." The running game will still be viewed as über-important, a high value will still be placed on speed, and players will continue being timed from home to first and in the 60-yard dash. More pro and college teams utilize the running game than those that don't. However, a few changes have started to seep into showcase format. A couple of years ago, Perfect Game no longer required pitchers to run and be timed. For a long time, hurlers were expected to provide running times as well as position players, but no longer. "Billy-ball" is still revered, and Billy in this case doesn't derive from the Oakland A's general manager's moniker, but from the late, fiery Billy Martin.

Being able to hit will also continue to be emphasized in the skills portion of showcases, and it should be. It's just too bad that knowledge and proper use of the strike zone isn't a priority as well, at least in my opinion. This ignores the accomplishments and skills of a number of players with college and professional potential and takes them out of the loop to a large degree. Players who have talent but don't have the kind of bodies perhaps that are conducive to "selling jeans." The kind of player that Billy Beane likes. The player who is judged on his results, not how he looks.

Then again, there may not be as big a rift as imagined. One of the clubs held up as the leading "anti–Billy Beane" club, i.e., an organization that has the reputation among the general public as ignoring college players and focusing almost exclusively on high school talent, is the Atlanta Braves. But this may be a huge misconception and, according to the Braves' scouting director Roy Clark, is absolutely not the situation.

Patrick Ebert, a staff writer for Perfect Game, asked Clark that very question in an interview available on the Perfect Game website. Ebert asked, "So much is made about the high school versus college debate these days. Given your preference for high school players, do you believe it's not about drafting high school versus college players, but drafting the right player?"

Clark's reply is revealing. He said, "There's no question about it. When we go into that draft room, we don't sit there and line up one board and say, 'Okay, here's all the college guys that we're not going to take and here are the high school guys that we are.' We try to take the best players. In 2001 we took a guy named Richard Lewis from Georgia Tech. Absolutely loved him, his ability, his makeup, and we slotted him accordingly and we took him in the sandwich round. The next year we took Dan Meyer, the guy we just traded to Oakland for Tim Hudson. We've taken a lot of college guys over the years, a lot more than people think. However, with so many teams concentrating solely on college players, there's very few of those guys left for us. We like that because more and more of the better high school guys are slipping to us, and deeper. So, we're getting what we feel like are second- and third-round high school guys in the fourth and fifth round. I know Logan White (Los Angeles Dodgers), Jack Zduriencik (Milwaukee Brewers) and other scouting directors that are known to take high school guys are loving that, too."

— 14 —

Select and Travel Teams:
The Other Major Force at Work
in the New World of Baseball

One more major element arrived to change the landscape of youth base-ball in the form of travel or "select" teams.

Such teams have been around for decades in one form or another. In the fifties and sixties, for instance, semi-pro teams proliferated the landscape and were the early forerunners of select teams. My uncle Bill Edgerton, a left-handed pitcher who played for five major league teams, mostly in the minors, played on such a team when he was in high school, the South Bend Sherman Cleaners, in a league composed of similar teams in northern Indiana and southern Michigan. Bill's team was composed of high school stars such as himself, along with ex-college and ex-pro players.

Travel teams have a long and storied history. However, what we consider travel teams today—comprised of players of high school age and younger—emerged about thirty years ago. At the onset, they were few and scattered and made up, for the most part, of superior talent.

Along about the same time as the emergence of the Little League World Series as a nationally televised phenomena and with the advent of mega-salaries begun by A-Rod's historic contract, travel teams began to take shape as a true force in youth baseball and for the same reasons that showcases emerged as major forces upon the landscape. Initially, they, like the original travel teams, were made up of the very best players, often recruited from out-side the geographical area in which they were based. But very quickly, as more and more people became aware of these teams and saw how the players began to get noticed by scouts, especially by the pros and a few of the more astute college programs, they began springing up everywhere. In the past ten years or so, these teams have multiplied at unprecedented rates.

Scouts and college coaches congregate to watch a game at the 2007 BCS championships in Fort Myers, Florida.

And the quality of talent and competition is widely diverse. The more parents became aware of these teams and discovered that being on such a team could help little Johnny in his quest for stardom (meaning becoming a high draft pick or obtaining a ride to a top DI program), more of these parents began forming their own travel teams. A great many of these teams are nothing more than a glorified rec team all-star team and many aren't even at that level.

As these teams proliferated, more national organizations sprang up to accommodate them. Today, there are probably a couple dozen so-called "World Series" a young player can easily find himself playing in. Billed as "national" in scope, many of these organizations might have teams from as few as six or seven states. In more than one of these events, just belonging to the organization and paying the annual dues qualifies a team for their "World Series."

In what has become a common scenario, little Johnny's dad, miffed that his pride and joy wasn't selected as an all-star for whatever Little League or other rec league he played in, goes out and forms a travel team, centered, of course, around little Johnny. Teammates are mostly other "Little Johnnys" who weren't picked by the same league either.

Most of these teams will have tryouts and purportedly select the best of the crop, but often, the coaches evaluating the hopefuls are the same coaches that plied their craft in the local daddyball league. The force behind the majority of them — why they were formed in the first place — is a father trying to provide a platform for his son. Most of these teams die a natural death in a few years. Their demise usually coincides with the moment the son either gives up baseball (or has it given up for him when not selected for a scholarship or taken in the draft), or when the dream is actually achieved and the boy moves on to the next level. If there are younger brothers still coming up, the team may hang around until that player's baseball future has been determined. Some teams last longer. A few of the founders of such teams really enjoy baseball and have a genuine desire to help out young players. Or, sometimes an organization is successful financially or even on the field of play and continues fielding teams because of those factors.

This certainly does not describe all travel teams, just the majority of squads that have littered the baseball landscape in the past few years.

When they first began, for the most part, such teams truly were "elite." Teams like the Houston Heat, the Central Florida Renegades, the Katy (TX) Sting, Indiana Yankees, the East Cobb teams, Chet Lemons Juice were far superior to rec ball teams.

However, very quickly it seems, a host of other teams sprang up that were "select" in name only.

R.W. "Bob" Miller, father of Quinton, one of the highest ranked high school players in the country (as a junior, ranked #4 for his 2008 class by Perfect Game) has seen the gamut of travel teams.

He relates: "We might have a bit of a unique perspective on travel ball because Quinton started playing travel baseball when we lived in California between the ages of nine to twelve. While in California you could find five good travel teams in a ten-mile radius. We then moved to New Jersey where at first we thought we were in the black hole of baseball. However, the changes in the northeast for the so-called 'better' players have improved dramatically over the last few years. There are now top-level travel teams in New Jersey [Tristate Arsenal, Farrah Builders, Baseball U] that are very competitive on a national level at many of the Perfect Game and national AAU events. From what I can see, the most talented kids are moving away from in-town or rec baseball [Little League, Cal Ripken, Babe Ruth, Legion, etc.] and are signing up with travel teams that will play against better competition.

"At the younger levels, I believe some of the reasons are not always the right ones. Dad isn't happy because Johnny didn't make the all-star teams so 'I will start up my own travel club.'" "However, some do it because they are bored with the archaic rules of Little League and other similar rec leagues. No lead-offs, no on-pitch stealing, lesser base path and pitching distances, etc. I believe at the older levels this is primarily due to the fact that these players aspire to play at the next level, be it college or pro, and Legion or Babe Ruth doesn't cut it.

"We have also seen a greater focus on getting our players seen at a more local level in New Jersey as well," Miller says. "There is a fairly new program called the New Jersey Super 17's [two years old in 2007] that brings in most of the top 17U players to form a scout league consisting of six teams [two south, two central, two north]. These teams play primarily in the mornings two to three days a week throughout July. This gives college and pro teams a chance to watch three games in a row that includes most of the best talent in New Jersey. In the past, a recruiter or pro scout would travel to New Jersey to see a player or two—now in the same time expended he can watch 120 top players in one day! Most stay for the week and leave with a pretty good idea of what is available in New Jersey. Needless to say, this has helped many of our players to get more exposure/scholarships already, and I would imagine over the last two years as well as into future years, you will see a much greater number of New Jersey talent going to bigger and better baseball schools.

"Is this working? It may be too early to tell, however, from our personal experience it has been a great recourse. New Jersey baseball people are doing a much better job of getting the better players seen by those who make the baseball decisions."

Miller likes what they're doing in New Jersey as far as better travel teams and in providing opportunities for kids in the state to be seen by colleges and the pros, but he saves his top praise for Perfect Game, perhaps natural since it was Perfect Game that got Quinton on the national radar.

"Regarding Perfect Game, I am afraid I will be one of those that might be accused of 'drinking the Kool-Aid' so to speak. My son has only done one Perfect Game showcase [2005 Perfect Game Underclass National in Fort Myers]. However, he has played in, I believe, three Perfect Game WWBA events. The bottom line is this ... there is no other company that puts on better events or that will get your son exposed to the right baseball people as Perfect Game." For the record, Quinton has attended and participated in a number of other showcase venues from other companies.

Miller continues. "Not only are they good at providing quality events, these guys actually seem to care about these kids. I'll share a personal story about Jerry Ford with you.

"First, a little background. Quinton was already ranked pretty high in his class by Perfect Game [fourth]. He had been to quite a few events [Perfect Game and non–Perfect Game] over the summer and fall, and I was at the point of asking myself, when is enough, enough? On top of this, he had just received an invitation to attend the Perfect Game Underclass Showcase again, which is held in December. By the way — the National Underclass showcase is the biggest underclass event of the year for underclassmen. The invite happened to come just before we left for the October WWBA 18U event in Jupiter, so this is where my story begins.

"I happened to run into Jerry Ford at the WWBA event in Jupiter. I had conversed with him through the PG website message board a couple of times, however, I had never met him so I thought I'd introduce myself.

"Not only did Jerry take the time to say hello, he actually talked to me about baseball for at least fifteen minutes. You could tell he was genuinely excited about the event and how some of the players were performing. After a few minutes, I mentioned that it was hard to pick and choose which events you should attend to make sure your son had the exposure needed to being seen by the schools he was interested in. We also talked about the real possibility of overexposure for these kids. When he asked who my son was, I told him and he said he knew Quinton and had some very nice and specific things to say about him. Pretty cool thing to hear from someone as highly regarded as Jerry Ford! The PG Underclass showcase came up in our conversation and his response was that Quinton had already accomplished what he needed to with Perfect Game and recruiters, and he really didn't think he needed to be at the PG Underclass this year. In fact, he said he thought it would probably do him some good to rest his arm and get ready for the next year. Now it would have been easy for him to tell me that if my son wanted to be considered for AFLAC or the PG National next year he should be at the PG Underclass, but he said, in essence, save your money and let your boy rest. On top of this, in a follow-up email a couple of weeks later, he gave me some great advice about what to expect next year, and then took the time to write up a list of events he thought my son should focus on attending next year and to contact him if I had any questions about anything. His final line in his message summed it up for me. It said, 'Feel free to contact me any time. Kids like your son are the very reason I do what we do.' I actually believe him, because as they say — actions speak louder than words."

As much as Perfect Game and other showcases have done for his son, Miller still offers a cautionary note. "Is there a down side to the whole showcase/tournament phenomena? I believe there is. I do think that there are a lot of people spending too much money hoping to buy a dream. If you go to one event you can get a pretty good read on where you stack up against the competition. Tournaments are one thing, but showcases are often overdone. To send your kid to four, five, six showcases over a period of two years is just too much and not needed, in my opinion.

"The bottom line is this: there are none better at what they do than

Perfect Game, and they are providing a much-needed service to everyone involved — the players, the colleges, and the pros. I hear too many people say that Perfect Game is in it for the money. Well, if they make some money, good for them. In my short time working with PG, it just isn't the case. I believe it is in the best interest of everyone that's involved in amateur baseball to keep a company like Perfect Game profitable so it can continue to do what it does."

John Wilhelmsen and his son Tom had a different experience with select teams. Although John had coached Little League for ten years, Pony League, coached a team in the Youth Olympic Tournament in Tucson, Arizona, and had been a volunteer pitching coach at Tucson High School for eight years, he was somewhat skeptical of travel and select teams, not having much experience with them. He relates how his mind was changed.

"I was sitting at my desk ready to close out the day. It was Monday and my wife was out of town and I needed to get home to cook and clean. My 16-year-old son Tom called and told me he had just gotten a phone call and some guy wanted him to pitch in Florida on Friday. He said the guy's name was Jerry Ford and he was calling from Perfect Game and that he wanted Tom to pitch for a team called Baseball America. [The event was the 2000 Perfect Game Wood Bat World Championship.]

"Tom's older brother Erik had played varsity baseball at Tucson High School, and I recalled him getting a letter asking him to join a team to play in Australia. Just pay $2,500.00 to join this team. I thought this offer from Perfect Game was also a scam. I had never heard of them or of their Wooden Bat Championship event.

"I called J.J. Hardy [J.J. and Tom played Little League and Pony League together], figuring that he might know something about Perfect Game. J.J. assured me that Perfect Game was legitimate and that he was playing for Team California at the same event. He told me that Jerry Ford was the boss at Perfect Game and that I could believe anything that Mr. Ford told me.

"I called Mr. Ford and he told me that Tom would be met at the airport, taken to a hotel, and would have rides to and from the fields, and then would be taken back to the airport on Monday. After a few calls to my wife in New York, we decided that this would be a good opportunity for Tom, and although we were apprehensive about allowing Tom to travel by himself, I called Mr. Ford and told him that Tom would be there.

"We didn't have cell phones at the time, so I called Mr. Ford every day. He filled me in on Tom's activities, his play and his team's success. He knew what Tom was doing and whom he was doing it with. We talked about baseball, coaching and kids. I never felt rushed; he always had time to assure me that Tom was eating and sleeping and having a good time. I never realized how busy Mr. Ford was during this time.

"Tom got to pitch a few innings early in the event. Mr. Ford told me that Tom did well and would end up starting a game on Monday. Tom started a semifinal game versus East Cobb and J.J. was the starting pitcher of the other semifinal game against Team Canada. This was one of my highlights as a Little League coach, having two boys from our Little League pitching in the semifinals. Oh, how I wished that I were there! Tom was pulled after a few innings and a few runs allowed. His team ended up winning and then beat Team California for the championship.

"I picked Tom up at the airport in Phoenix, and Tom was really excited about the time that he had. On the way home to Tucson, he told me how the first day the Paganetti family adopted him, picking him up, taking him to lunch and dinner. After that, he was in the company of Dmitri Young and Sean Casey, who were assistant coaches of his team. He told me about his new friends, Scott Kazmir and Delmon Young; how cool it was to pitch to Langdon Powell, how good Jeremy Sowers and Kevin Guyette pitched and how Billy Paganetti was a hitting machine. He was also very excited about the fact that Disney was making a movie about his coach, Jim Morris [of *The Rookie* book and movie fame, who was a coach for Perfect Game teams while he was playing pro ball].

"He told me one of the highlights of his trip; one night some parents took Tom and several other boys to a block party in Palm Beach. There were bands on each end of the block and they had a great time."

Tom Wilhelmsen was drafted by the Milwaukee Brewers in the seventh round of the 2002 MLB draft. He retired from professional baseball on Father's Day, 2005. His father said that he spent more time on the disabled list than he did as an active player. "Today, Tom is doing well," John said. "His smile is back on his face and he is becoming a responsible young man. He works as a bartender and is planning to marry his high school sweetheart."

John Wilhelmsen retired from coaching baseball in May 2007 and today devotes himself to the growth of his business so he can sell it and retire. "Then," he said, "I hope to get back into baseball in some capacity."

— 15 —

Perfect Game's People

What follows are Jerry Ford's assessments about some of the people he feels are most responsible for the company's success.

Betty Ford: Betty Ford appears frequently in this book and that's because she's a major part of the driving force behind the company. Jerry Ford freely admits he could have achieved little without her. About his wife, Jerry says, "My wife, Betty, is the hardest-working person I've ever known. She's always supported whatever I do, knowing that I was never going to be rich." Likewise, two of Jerry and Betty's sons, Andy and Ben, are both included in this book and both play significant roles in the company. The Fords have two other children who are not involved in the day-to-day operation but still "help when they can," according to Jerry. The Fords' oldest son, Nick, is a retired U.S. Navy officer who works for a firm that inspects nuclear operations. Jerry says, "I'm very proud of Nick's accomplishments and he still talks to his mother just about every day." Ford says his daughter, Jenny, does the same. "Jenny's an outstanding floral designer and owns a floral shop in Connecticut that is very successful," he says. And Jenny, like Nick, still finds time to talk to her mother every day, "sometimes several times a day," Jerry says.

Tyson Kimm: "Tyson is one of the owners and just like Andy and Jason, he has been through hell and back with Perfect Game. These guys just never give up! Might not say much for their intelligence, but it speaks volumes about their persistence and loyalty. I've been a 'loyalty-above-all-else' person. Of course, it helps when that loyalty also has a lot of talent, like these guys do. I really don't care if I ever have a lot of money myself — too busy to enjoy it anyhow — but I do hope that someday these guys are stinkin' rich because they truly deserve it!"

Jim Arp: "Jim is one of the most important people in our entire organization. Anyone who knows him will admit exactly that. There is no one on earth that enjoys helping kids and doing things the right way more than Jim.

He is in charge of players and there's nothing more critical at Perfect Game than what he does. He probably talks to more parents than anyone in baseball. That's not always a lot of fun, but he is honest with them."

Taylor McCoullough: "He started as an intern and now he is one of the most important people in our organization. Taylor is in charge of our tournament division which includes a couple of WWBA events that include 148 teams each. We won't be able to keep him much longer; a big league front office is in his future. There have already been inquiries."

Steve James: "Steve runs our Iowa Leagues, among other duties. He is another guy who will go out of his way to help deserving players. Steve is also our resident artist, designing many of the covers for programs and brochures."

Nancy Lain: "Nancy's my sister, but helps run the office at Perfect Game. She has lots of experience as an administrator, but her greatest attribute is how much she cares. She spends a lot of time talking to parents, some happy, some not."

David Mixon: "David runs our tech department. He is very talented and once decided to take another job with a big firm and after one day at that new job — I'm not kidding — he came back to Perfect Game. He is a guy you can call at 3 A.M. if there's something important. He now has grown to love the game as much as the rest of us."

Jim VanScoyac: "Jim is in charge of individual instruction for Perfect Game. He is a legendary high school coach from our state [he also coached in professional baseball]. He has the most wins of any high school coach in the state of Iowa, mostly at tiny Norway High School, and his character was a large part of the story in the recently released film, *Final Season*."

Tom Jackson: "Tom joined us many years ago and handles all the merchandise and equipment for PG and the PG Pro Shop. He's one of the most well-liked guys in our organization. He is another great representative for all of us with his low key, easy-going personality. He's also the resident wildlife chef at PG. He hunts, fishes, cooks, and then feeds us!"

Kirk Gardner: "The PG scouting supervisor, and he runs PG Wisconsin. There just aren't enough people in baseball like Kirk. He is unbelievably competitive, but in every case he simply loves helping young baseball players succeed. Yes, he wants the very best players to attend the bigger PG events and he takes it personally if they don't. However, it's because he really believes they should and he wants them to experience it. Kirk is not a 'credit taker'— he is a worker with an unbelievable passion for the game. If we have 99 out of the top 100 players in the country, he will be pissed off about the one who isn't there."

Gary Koeppel: "Gary is PG's marketing director. He has lots of experience, but more importantly, he too, fits the profile of the typical PGer.

Baseball is highly addictive and being a former college player and on the board of the Cedar Rapids Professional Club, it only was natural to join forces with the other low key, big baseball nuts in town."

Billy Nicholson: "Billy is a high school coach in Georgia who has worked PG events for many summers. He might be the best batting practice pitcher in the country, among other things. He has coached the AFLAC East team the past two years."

Mike Spiers: "Mike runs California for us. He is much like Kirk Gardner in that he is very competitive and wants the very best players to attend PG events. He also coaches the ABD Bulldogs, one of the top summer and fall teams in the country."

Rob Bruno: "Rob runs the NorCal program in Northern California. Rob has shared so many great ideas with me it would be impossible to remember them all. He's always been a big supporter and I hope that continues for a long time."

Cecil Espy: "Cecil has been a big supporter for a long time. A former MLB player, he now spends his time working with high school kids in Texas. He and Omar Washington have coached in the AFLAC game since the very beginning."

Garth Iorg: "Garth is a former MLB player and coach who owns the Knoxville Yard [of Tennessee]. He has supported us for many years and helped us in many ways. Garth is truly one of the good guys in baseball. He coached in the first AFLAC Game."

Omar Washington: "A longtime baseball personality and coach from Texas, Omar has always supported PG. He has coached the West AFLAC Team [along with Cecil Espy] in every Classic since the beginning."

Jimmy Zellman: "Jimmy is our Minnesota man. He is one of the PG coaches that players like the most. Like so many of the people we know, Jimmy just loves trying to help young baseball players."

Brad Tremetiere: "Big Brad is yet another guy who has supported us so much for many years. He is a great scout and can recognize talent in a heartbeat, but with him it's not a job — he loves it."

Dick Vaske: "Dick is a hardcore hardworking PG supporter who has helped us for years with things no one else wanted anything to do with. Like sell things. He travels all over the country setting up souvenir tents at all our events. Dick is the real person they were thinking about when they wrote the song *My Way*."

Eric Oliver: "Eric is a coach/teacher who has worked only part-time over the past several years. He has made a great impression on our facility within the Cedar Rapids community. He has been instrumental in working on our 'Create a Fan' program for young kids."

Wes Penick: "Royals scout and former Perfect Game scout. Wes was a great representative for PG in his years with us. Always polite and conducted himself with class. The Royals are very lucky."

Andrea Bachman: "She spent many years helping Perfect Game in so many ways. Everyone liked her very much, both co-workers and customers."

Greg Sabers: "Young guy and he's a guy who is most comfortable on the road. We tell Greg you need to be in California tomorrow and he's actually elated. He fits the mold and will be a great scout."

Kyle Noessen: "Also a young guy with outstanding talent. Kyle is ready to do anything asked of him. He, too, will become a great scout."

Tom Battista: "Braves' scout and former PG scout. Still a very close friend and supporter. Tom was a superstar at PG. If we had a PG Hall of Fame, he would be a unanimous choice. I can't thank him enough for the years he dedicated to us. My scouting report for Tom Battista would end with a comment I use for very special talents ... the sky is the limit!"

Blaine Clemmens: "Braves scout and former PG scout. Blaine was one of our main people and he is extremely talented. In fact, he could easily be a sports writer if he ever decides to give up scouting. He has great baseball knowledge and passion for the game."

Tim Buss: "Tim devoted his life to us during the first few years of Perfect Game. He was a little guy who played for me in college [outstanding shortstop]. He started working with the head trainer for the Iowa Cubs club at our facility in Des Moines. Tim was a guy that everyone liked immediately. I knew he was going to be successful even if we weren't. These days he sits in the Chicago Cubs dugout. He is their head strength and conditioning guy."

Ray Stefani: "Our attorney who helped us when we couldn't pay, just because he believed in what we were doing and he loved kids and baseball."

John Wylde: "I could write a book and someone sure needs to. John helped us get popular in the northeast. He is a legend in the Cape Cod League and the Wareham Gatemen. He has given so much to baseball. I'll just say he's the nicest man I've ever met!"

Brad Clement: "Coach and dad of Jeff [first round, Mariners]. We can't thank Brad enough for the years he spent coaching and helping PG. when he retires, I hope he joins us. He is one of the true class acts in baseball."

Patrick Ebert: "Contributing writer and all-around great guy. He is a true baseball nut who fits in perfectly with us."

Cam Walker: "A college coach and former pro player, Cam helped us an awful lot in so many ways over the years."

Bruce Hotchkiss: "Another former pro player, a businessman, and just a great person who lost a lot of sleep worrying about Perfect Game."

Rick Mathews: "An MLB coach for the Rockies who really inspired us by his own work ethic example and tremendous knowledge of the game."

Clay Hansen: "Clay was a giant supporter of PG right from the beginning and he also happens to be one of the nicest people I've ever met."

Curt Long: "Curt was the head coach at Mount Mercy who decided I might be able to help a little. He is a guy who taught me a lot about class."

Tony Damewood: "Tony was the head coach at Iowa Wesleyan who allowed a crazy coach [me!] to do his thing. We sure had a lot of fun.... I can't thank Tony enough for all of his support."

Joel Lepel: "The Twins minor league director and former CrossChecker who I truly enjoyed working with. One of the best baseball people I've ever met. He kept us on our toes in the early years."

Dan Jennings: "The Marlins' vice president and former D-Rays scouting director, Dan has said so many good things about us to other baseball people and has been a tremendous friend, both to me and to Perfect Game. He probably doesn't even know how much he's helped us."

Tim Wilkin: "The Cubs scouting director and former Blue Jay scouting director, Tim was the very first scouting director to start following what we were doing at Perfect Game, and I'll never forget him being quoted saying good things about us when no one else knew who we were."

Mike Stouffer: "Phillies scout and former college coach we owe a lot to for being so damned entertaining as well as helping us whenever we would ask."

*   *   *

"There are just so many people who've helped us over the years and to whom we owe a great debt to," Ford said. "I know I'll forget somebody, but just a few of those include Jim Pransky, Tim Kelly, Mitch Webster, Harvey Kuenn, Bob Oldis, Jerry Lafferty, Terry Tripp, Joe Robinson, Steve Foster, Stan Zalenski, Dave Karif, Mike Grouse, Jeff Cornell, and all the other scouts who were so important to our success right from the beginning. And, there are the folks in other venues who've worked with us in venues all over the country. Gary Ewen, John Yarbrough, and Jeff Milke in Fort Myers have bailed us out of spots many, many times over the years. Jack Roeder [general manager of the Cedar Rapids Kernels] has helped us so much in our home town. Al Johnson from AFLAC has been great to work with and it has been lots of fun.

"Perfect Game didn't happen by accident. It didn't happen because of one or even a few people. It took people from all over the country who shared our vision.

"Of course, the people most responsible for our success are the thousands of players and parents who have touched us over the past 15 years. If I may say one thing, I'd like to give a great *big* thank-you to one of my former players who chose to ignore my expert advice. I once told Kurt Warner I thought he had a much better future if he concentrated on baseball.

"I guess that just proves no one is infallible."

Kentaro Yasutake

Illustrative of how the Perfect Game "family" was formed is the story of how Kentaro Yasutake, PG's international scouting coordinator. A native of Japan, Yasutake played college ball at Emporia State and in his senior year, decided he wanted to stay in the States and get a job in baseball. Upon the advice of his coach, he phoned Jerry Ford and asked for a job.

Jerry Ford takes obvious pride in relating the story. "Kentaro called at the worst possible time. It was during the period when we were facing bankruptcy and had absolutely no money, especially for hiring someone. I was upfront in telling Kentaro this, but it didn't dissuade him in the least. Finally I told him that if he could get to Cedar Rapids, I'd at least interview him, but because

Kentaro Yasutake takes a break at the 2007 WWBA World Championships in Jupiter, Florida, to pose for a photograph. He maintains the company website and keeps in touch with international correspondents, among other duties.

of our financial situation it would most likely be a fruitless trip for him.

"When I met him, I could see right away that this was a special kid. I told him again that we couldn't afford to pay someone, and his reply was that he really didn't care about money—that he'd work for nothing. He didn't hesitate a second, but just jumped on the 'opportunity' I was offering him.

"His attitude sold him. I told him we might be able to pay him a thousand a month but there was no guarantee of how long we could even pay that—at that time, we weren't even sure we'd remain in business that much longer. He said he'd take it and was grateful for the opportunity. It was plain he was passionate about working for us—he'd even slept in the heap he'd driven up the night before as he didn't have enough money for a room and wanted to be on time for our interview."

He began work the next day, on September 1, 2001.

"Kentaro is the humblest person you could ever meet," Jerry went on. "He'd never tell you any of this." And he hadn't. During perhaps a dozen interviews and conversations with Kentaro, he'd never mentioned anything about himself nor how he'd come to work for the organization.

He turned out to not only be an astute baseball man, but a tireless worker. Jerry related what he said was a typical "Kentaro story." The company had sent him that first year to Joplin, Missouri, to cover the USA Tournament of Stars and as it happened, Joplin was experiencing a record-breaking heat wave. There were over 300 scouts in attendance and it got so hot that the scouts left the field to seek out shade. Only one guy, Kentaro, remained with his radar gun. He stayed for the entire game and afterward all the rest of the scouts lined up to get the game info from him, which he gave out graciously. "This is a kid just out of college and he showed what he was made of, earning the respect of all the older men immediately," Ford said.

Kentaro's acumen as a guy with a serious talent for judging ballplayers and their potential became evident immediately. Jerry says, "The Atlanta Braves tried to hire him as a scout early on, and, fortunately for us, they were unable to as he was experiencing problems with his work visa and citizenship papers with the government and was unable to take advantage of their offer.

"I really hesitate to designate any one individual as my 'right-hand man,'" Jerry said, "as a lot of my people would qualify as such. But if forced to, I'd probably have to name Kentaro."

In talking to Kentaro himself, he said very little about himself, but was quick to point out the merits of others.

Asked by my Tristate University student researcher Mitch Harshbarger about his qualifications when he began to work at Perfect Game, Yasutake said, "My qualifications for the job were being a former college baseball player, finishing my career as a pitcher at Emporia State University. Also, I brought a unique perspective to the company after playing baseball both in Japan as well as the U.S."

Asked about his early work, he said, "The first couple of months went really fast as I was learning how all the systems worked and finding out what I could do to help the company. My original responsibilities including evaluating players at events and organizing information after those events were over. I was impressed with everybody with not only how hard they worked but how much fun we had, too."

He continues to have fun. When asked to describe any low points in his years with the organization he couldn't recall any. Highlights? A lot, it seems. "When I started with PG, there were fewer than 15 employees and 12 events total. Now there are forty-plus full-time employees [hundreds of others, part-time] and over a hundred events. There are still the four original members of the staff that have been here since day one and they still work as hard as they did years ago. These are just great people to work with."

His typical day? "There's never a typical day! I have a wide variety of duties pertaining to IT work. Some of those responsibilities include maintaining the website, updating player profiles, constantly developing new website designs, maintaining the PG database and developing the new website/database which will integrate all websites and player/team data in one location. I maintain consistent contact with international correspondents to stay informed of the top baseball players outside the United States."

Scouting prowess and personnel

The ability to accurately access young ballplayer's five tools and to project where a player will be in the future, skill-wise and body-wise, is a skill only acquired by a relative few. The personnel from Perfect Game, the pros and college officials agree, are unparalleled in those abilities. Scouts from pro ball need to have a good idea of where a young man will be in three to five years, while it's important to college coaches to be able to predict where a high school player will be in two to three years.

A lot of factors go into these determinations. Body type is important, and often the boy's parents will be considered to help gauge what kind of a frame a 17- or 18-year-old boy will grow into in the next few years.

A large part of Perfect Game's success stems from the personnel. Character is of primary importance when Ford considers hiring someone in a non-technical position such as in the computer field (although, most of their technical and business people also possess a sound background and knowledge of baseball). The second requirement is a genuine desire to help young men achieve their baseball dreams; and third is the ability to judge playing skills.

Typical of a Perfect Game employee is the history of Dan Kennedy, Perfect Game's northeast director. He relates his own story:

"I began to work for Perfect Game in 2002. I joined them because Tommy Battista, a scout for the Atlanta Braves, had contacted me about players from Team Connecticut, which I'd started in 1994. [Team Connecticut has won five national championships since then.] They [the Braves] were looking for a place for their [northeast area] premier players to play in the summer. Perfect Game made it possible for good northeastern players to get the looks they deserved, which wasn't likely before they came on the scene. Because of the weather, we were a neglected part of the country.

"I had a good baseball background. I'd played college baseball and then played pro ball with the Cubs, Red Sox and the Orioles; mostly, I was a career minor leaguer!

Players wait their turn in the battle cages during a rain delay at the 2006 PG Academic Showcase in Fort Myers, Florida.

"What attracted me to Perfect Game [and vice versa] was that they respected the game of baseball and they were completely honest. They never lie, they never inflate the numbers. Above all, they try always to be honest with the kids and scouts respect the honesty.

"Perfect Game is unlike any other organization of its kind. They open their arms and let you in just like you're family. That's what it is—a family. I'm just very pleased to be part of it."

Jerry Ford is in the catbird's seat behind home plate at Schott Field at the University of Cincinnati during the 2007 PG National Showcase.

come — there have been plenty of lighter moments and incidents. The best story is about a player who took the field under an alias.

As Jerry Ford relates the story: "A couple of agents had been working on the behalf of Hall-of-Famer Ted Williams' son John Henry to get him into the WWBC on a team. Ted was in bad health at the time and the agents were telling me that this was something John Henry really wanted to do for his dad. As a kid he hadn't gotten into baseball much, but now that his dad was in failing health, he wanted to give professional ball a shot to make his father proud. Up to now, he'd been involved in his father's autograph and memorabilia business. But he'd been working out for several months with trainers, and he felt that his ability was good enough that if the right person saw him play he would get a chance, and the word was that his agents had heard the PG National Showcase was the best place to be seen by the right people.

"His agents approached us with their request and my answer was an unqualified 'No.' I kept saying no; it'd make a farce out of the whole thing. At the time, he was 32 years old! They kept after me and kept after me and I kept saying no. I told them there were plenty of other things we could do for him to get him seen by pro scouts but they said no. Their big thing was they didn't want anyone to know who he was — that was their whole issue. John Henry wanted to make it on his own, not because of his father. To make a long story short, I changed my mind — allowed it to happen. We gave him the fictitious name of 'William Johnson' and put him on one of the teams and didn't tell anyone. In fact, until this minute, we still hadn't told hardly anyone.

"Well, he's out there playing and he looks pretty good ... not good enough [to be signed] ... but pretty good. He was really a good athlete. It came time for him to take batting practice and by God — *there was Ted Williams as a right-handed batter!* If you'd ever seen Ted Williams' approach at the plate, you'd say that was Ted Williams! Everybody was there — Dan Jennings, Roy Clark — all the top scouts — and I'm not telling anybody who it is — and people kept saying, 'Who's that remind you of? Who's that look like?' There just aren't any kids today who hit like that — those low hands — and he really stood out. When he stepped up there, he looked like he'd hit ten out, but he didn't. Hit solid line drives. He looked okay, but nothing extraordinary.

"Then, when he played in the field, he looked okay, played harder than anyone else. He hustled everything out. He really didn't do that well, but he played harder than anybody else. He also got along great with the players and then they started wondering who he was. He was really a good-looking man. The players started to figure out he was much older and wondered if this was all a setup of some kind — if he was some movie star or something. I mean he was exceptionally good-looking — could easily have passed as a movie star.

"As it worked out — the Red Sox did sign him and gave him a chance and he played, I think A ball, as a 32-year-old rookie. Played a year or so and the Red Sox eventually figured out it was pretty futile. They'd signed him more to honor Ted than anything else, and really, that was all he and everyone else wanted — to do it for his dad more than anything else. Shortly after that, his dad died and then John Henry died himself, not long after."

Jerry paused, and then sighed. "John Henry was just like Ted only bigger and stronger — he had a bigger body. In fact, he might have been a great player, but he just never got into baseball when he was young."

Roger Clemens and his son Kobe

Jerry Ford recalls Roger Clemens. "When Roger's son Kobe played on a team that actually won the Jupiter tourney — the year we had the hurricane and moved it to Fort Myers — there had been a bunch of news stories earlier in the year about Roger causing problems at a Little League game. Once again, as in Wade Boggs' and other cases, it was a matter of extreme competitiveness. Kobe Clemens was on Phil Cross's Houston Heat team and played third base. It was during the major league playoffs and Roger's Houston Astros had just lost to the St. Louis Cardinals [he'd pitched and took the loss], allowing the Cardinals to go to the World Series. The next day after the loss, Roger was in Fort Myers to see his son play. He was interviewed and said that even if they'd won the game against St. Louis and gone to the Series, he'd already made arrangements with the Astros to be at Kobe's game. He was a really nice guy. He came through the front gate and even though he was helping coach the team [coaches and players don't pay admission fees], Roger and his wife drove through the gate and Betty was there and he paid and there was nothing about 'I'm Roger Clemens' or 'I'm the coach' or anything like that.

"There was a line of people during the game getting his autograph, and Roger was accommodating them and we heard about it and went over and roped off the area. He's really a good guy and so is Doug Drabeck whose son was also playing — both just the nicest, regular guys. Roger had all kinds of good things to say about the tournament.

"Oddly enough, as things went on — everybody trying to get photos with him and autographs — and Phil Cross came over to me and said, 'Roger Clemens wants to meet you.' I said, 'Bullshit!' and Phil said, 'No, I'm dead serious, Jerry. Roger wants to meet you.' Funny thing, my son Ben was playing with the Yankees at the same time Roger was. The reason Ben got called up to the major league club was that Roger had been put on the DL. That's kind of how he knew who I was as he'd heard about the Perfect Game thing from Ben.

"Anyway, I met him and he was really the nicest guy. He acted like I was more important than he was.' I told him my son was with the Yankees, and Roger said, 'Yeah, I know Ben. Really good kid.' He's really just the nicest, down-to-earth guy."

Pete Rose

"Pete Rose was supposed to come to our Jupiter tournament one year," Ford said. "He'd just made a video on hitting and he and his agent wanted to promote it and wanted us to bend over backwards to promote it. They were asking for things that were really out of kilter, and so we turned it down, as much as we would have loved to have had Pete there."

Jason Gerst stories

Jason Gerst has dozens of stories based on his experiences as a long-time Perfect Game employee and part-owner. About Tampa Bay's Carl Crawford, he says, "Carl Crawford flew up from Texas when he was a senior to attend our National Pre-Draft Showcase in the spring of 1999. Carl is one of the most athletic players, if not *the* most athletic, that I have ever seen at a Perfect Game event. I had the pleasure of driving him to the airport afterward and sharing a meal at Burger King before his flight left. I think he still owes me six bucks. He sure had a good appetite!"

One of Gerst's favorite success stories in which Perfect Game played a role is that of Zach Schreiber, a right-handed pitcher, who, Gerst said when Chris Wells interviewed him, had "just got moved up from AA to AAA last week." Gerst recalled the young man fondly. "As a junior in high school, Zach was a good athlete with lots of raw potential, but he played every sport. He was extremely intelligent and loved baseball. I remember seeing him as a sophomore thinking this kid has a chance if he keeps getting better, but I honestly didn't realize myself how good he could become. Then, during his junior year to senior year he started playing in our advanced leagues for the top players in Iowa and surrounding states [still another arm of Perfect Game is the spring and fall leagues for high school players in Iowa and Wisconsin]. The next year, he's topping out at 90 mph and bursting onto the scene. He went from a low-profile Iowa kid without any offers to going to Duke University on scholarship to play baseball. He did well at Duke and obviously received a great education in the process. I have never been so excited to see success for a player than Zach. We all at Perfect Game are big Zach Schreiber fans as you can imagine! His stats were lights out this year before going to Triple A, so I truly hope he makes the big leagues. It would be great for Zach and a great story."

Gerst's all-time favorite moment with Perfect Game was watching Scott Kazmir strike out the side in his second inning of work, topping out at 96. "He then asked me if he did okay. I replied, 'Yes, that was okay.'"

Gerst's favorite story involved one of Perfect Game's own "family," company business manager Don Walser's son Mitch. As Gerst recalls, "Mitch worked out at our indoor facility when he was about ten. The first time I saw him actually play, he was twelve and on a team called the Firebirds. They had some good players, but Mitch himself, I would honestly say, was an average to below-average 12-year-old. As time went on, I remember thinking he was too timid and had marginal tools. I didn't think baseball would be in his future. As time went on, Mitch did one thing more than I have ever seen from anyone else in my life. He hit and hit and hit and hit. Every single day. He truly is a self-made hitter. By the time he got to high school, he played in our scout league and continued to hit and hit good pitching. He went on to Kirkwood Community College after high school, where he was voted the team's MVP and led them in hitting. From there, he earned a scholarship to DII Upper Iowa University. In his final year there, he hit .427, a school record 64 RBIs, 11 home runs, 15 doubles.... The other interesting thing about Mitch is that he went from being a defensive liability to a good outfielder. He threw

87 mph at our pre-draft workout. He also went from being a high school freshman who ran over 8 seconds in the 60 to a 6.8 runner in college. All of us at Perfect Game really enjoyed watching him develop into a good baseball player who truly appreciates the game and got everything he could from his natural ability."

The Upton brothers

There have been many ballplayers who have participated in Perfect Game events and gone on to stellar careers in college and in the major league, but none have been bigger than B.J. and Justin Upton, who are the only brothers to have both been selected in the first round of the major league draft. B.J. was no. 2 overall in the 2002 draft to Tampa Bay, and the Arizona Diamondbacks chose younger brother Justin as the very first player in the 2005 draft.

When the boys' father, Manny Upton, was growing up, his dad nicknamed him "Bossman." When his eldest son was born, Manny's high school coach suggested he name the boy B.J. for "Bossman Junior," which he did. B.J.'s name on his birth certificate reads Melvin, but B.J. is what he goes by.

Manny starred in baseball and football at Norfolk State. When he graduated, he returned to the school to coach before taking a job scouting for the Chicago White Sox and the Kansas City Royals. Today, he works as a mortgage lender and has refereed college basketball for over a decade and a half in the Atlantic Coast Conference, plus three NCAA tournaments.

He told Perfect Game columnist Patrick Ebert that his oldest son, B.J., in particular, benefited from Perfect Game exposure. "Nobody knew about B.J. until he went to a Perfect Game event," he said. B.J.

B.J. Upton is pictured at the 2001 PG Nationals, the same year he was chosen no. 2 in the MLB draft. His PG report said "Upton is the #1 tools player in America for next year's draft" (courtesy Perfect Game USA).

echoed what his father said. "Perfect Game played a big part in my career. I think I went to four or five Perfect Game showcases and that got my name out there." Justin was recognized a bit earlier, as his older brother had paved the way for recognition. He also credits Perfect Game for much of his success, but feels his own emergence was due more, early on, to his performance during the Area Code games after his freshman year in high school. He gives Perfect Game a lot of credit, also, and attended seven Perfect Game events. Justin was also selected by Perfect Game to the AFLAC All-American game in 2004 and was presented with the first Jackie Robinson award as the AFLAC National High School Player of the year by Rachel Robinson and Cal Ripken.

I thought a perfect ending to this book would be to provide an interview with Manny Upton conducted by my Tristate University researcher, Dan Higginbotham. Manny Upton comes across as perhaps the "perfect" baseball dad — the kind of guy who creates a relationship with his sons that we all aspire to but most of the time fall short of.

But first, the back-story that involves the young man who conducted the interview for me, Dan Higginbotham.

It was just a few weeks into the spring semester classes at Tristate and I'd just asked for volunteers to conduct interviews for my research into the book for extra credit. I'd been meaning to contact Manny Upton for some time, but one thing after another interfered and I just hadn't gotten to a good time to pick up the phone and make the call.

Not only did every one of these engineering and computer-science and similar majored-students turn in excellent interviews and write-ups of them — talk about some bright kids— these young people were *great*— but in particular, Dan Higginbotham turned in a piece of journalistic interviewing that was downright masterful. His telephone interview with Manny Upton follows.

Dan: How did you first learn of Perfect Game?

Manny: Okay. I began my relationship with Perfect Game in 2001. B.J. attended their invitation camp for rising seniors and prospects [Perfect Game National Showcase], and I think that was the first year they had the top 100 prospect showcase. [Today, the top 200 seniors are invited.] It was in Tampa, Florida.

Dan: Did you go with your son? What was your initial impression of Perfect Game?

Manny: Yes, I went with him. It was impressive. B.J. was my first child to really get in the baseball scene, as he had been to the East Coast Showcase. Jerry [Ford] had brought in all the top players that were going to get drafted ... Scott Kazmir, Sergio Santos, Denard Span ... all of these guys who were in the top hundred. From there, B.J. went to the USA trial, and all the guys from the Perfect Game showcase were at the USA tryout. So Jerry did, and still does, a good job of getting all of the elite talent at his showcases.

Dan: So B.J. probably hadn't faced this level of competition before?

Manny: Exactly. Not in one setting. He may have seen one or two guys, other than the East Coast Showcase that he attended. At the time, the Perfect Game National Showcase was right after the draft, and it was all of the players who were going to be drafted the next year. Perfect Game was really one of B.J.'s first experiences with all of that talent in one place.

Dan: Was this the summer before B.J.'s senior year?

Manny: Yes, June of 2001, matter-of-fact. We get out of school late here [Chesapeake Bay, Virginia], so B.J. had to take a couple of days off of private school here.

Dan: What was B.J.'s initial impression?

Manny: He thought the competition was good. Any kid that's competitive wants to be in that environment, and it just gave him the opportunity to see what it would take to get to the level where he is now. He enjoyed it and it was a great experience. They put the guys up where they get to know

Some of the 160 golf carts used by scouts and college coaches cover the grounds at the 2007 WWBA World Championships in Jupiter, Florida (courtesy Perfect Game USA).

each other, and you basically begin lifelong relationships. He and Sergio Santos are still good friends.

Dan: Did B.J. attend more Perfect Game events?

Manny: Yeah. They have two of probably the top events for baseball. They had a wooden bat tournament that BJ and David Wright played in together [the WWBA National Championships held each year at the East Cobb Complex], being from this showcase scene [the same area — Chesapeake Bay]. That's probably the tournament that if you do well, you probably have a good chance of being drafted. Then, there's the tournament [WWBA World Championships in Jupiter, Florida] they hold in October, so that's a big event as well. But those are the two big events both B.J. and Justin attended.

Dan: What kind of exposure did B.J. get from this?

Manny: Every major league team has a representative at Perfect Game and every team will have somebody there at both events [Author's note: Most MLB teams have a large number of their scouts in attendance]. Some guys come out of the woodwork that they have never seen before, and they have a good showing. It certainly has an impact on their draft status, because you're talking about the elite group of kids in high school baseball, so it's going to have an impact on your draft status.

Dan: When did Justin first get involved with Perfect Game?

Manny: It was a little earlier [in his high school career], probably in 2003. Because after B.J. got drafted, he got some exposure, so his first Perfect Game activity was in 2003.

Dan: How did your two sons' experiences differ?

Manny: Justin's was different since he was B.J.'s brother, but he probably got treated — not as a prima donna, per se — but they knew who he was. So when Justin got on the scene, it was, 'Oh, there's B.J. Upton's brother.' From that standpoint, it was an easy transition for Justin because they knew who he was. Now Chesapeake was starting to get some notoriety as far as baseball players go. With B.J. coming from the area, along with Michael Cuddyer, when Justin popped on the scene, the transition was easier since they knew who he was and that kind of thing.

Dan: What was B.J. and Justin's greatest benefit from their Perfect Game experience?

Manny: The exposure. The competition. I think it's the highest level of competition, like the East Coast showcase that the scouts put on. I think, personally, that Perfect Game does the truly elite job for any high school player who wants to see where he stands against other high school players.

Dan: Is there anything you would like to see Perfect Game do a better job at? Do they have any areas for improvements?

Manny: Yeah, give me some more money to pay to go to their events [laughs]. I don't know how they can with the NCAA being so involved, but provide scholarships for kids who should be there but can't be there. I don't know how that would work with the NCAA. I know some kids who should have or could have done well there, but couldn't because of financial things. Other than that, they do an excellent job of getting kids exposure and they do a good job of getting the top kids there. You can't get every one of them, but I think they get probably 95 percent of the top kids in the country to their showcase, which says a lot for Jerry and his sons and the others.

Dan: Has Perfect Game changed at all during the time that you and your sons have been involved in it?

Manny: It's gotten bigger. When B.J came on the scene, it wasn't as big as it is now, but they've earned their credibility by their players, by their rankings, and with major league baseball and colleges. I think their credibility has certainly increased, but as far as anything bad, no. I haven't been involved in it the last couple of years, but I know what kind of people Jerry Ford and his sons are, and I've never had anything but good relationships with them, so I can only speak for my family's relationship with them. And that was prior to B.J.'s making it. I'm saying that when we initially got involved, they were fair, and that's all you ask. Some people are some kind of moneymakers, and Jerry came across to me as someone who has a true concern for his players. I have recommended players that they have never even seen, but they took my recommendation. So, anybody can call them if they see someone who they think they have a chance and they'll take an opportunity to look at them. They don't just take my word; they put their own work into it. They were trying to make sure their tournaments were run well and all of those things.

Dan: Do you wish there had been something like Perfect Game available to you when you were a young player?

Manny: Absolutely, I wish there were, but my parents and I couldn't have afforded it. That's what I'm saying about somehow somebody should be able to subsidize kids who live in the inner cities who want to be major league players but can't. If Major League Baseball or anyone wants to target these kids, then you have to subsidize some things for those kids.

Dan: There's been some criticism that Perfect Game caters to "rich, white boys." I wondered what your take on that is.

Manny: I don't think so! I can only speak for me, but any time I've recommended a player, and I've recommended some kids who weren't "rich, white boys," and I've recommended a lot of black kids who don't have that opportunity, and they've [Perfect Game] always been receptive to my recommendations. And I think that's baseball in general. I don't think they so much care about race. I think it's about being exposed and that's why I say there has to be some subsidies there that can allow kids to go to those types of camps. That's the biggest thing. I think Jerry would take anybody, but how can they get around the NCAA and their string of rules? I can name a lot of black kids who went through Perfect Game's programs, but I can only speak for the people who were involved with me. They were always fair with me, and I can't say anything different. I think Jerry would subsidize some kids to come — I don't think he'd have a problem with that. We've had that conversation, he and I, and he would like to reach out and do some things along those lines, but if a kid goes to college, it might jeopardize his eligibility. The general consensus about baseball is that you have to be "rich" because of showcases and equipment purchases. You can take one basketball and play with ten guys. You can take one football and play a football game. You can't do the same with baseball. Golf is the same way, but you can't make the comment, "Every minority kid can't play golf." Every *kid* [of any race] can't play golf, whether they're a minority or not. It's economics. You have to have a set of golf clubs, golf balls, golf shoes, and before you start playing golf, you've spent $600. Baseball is the same way. Before you start playing, you have to have a glove, shoes, and a bat. The last time I bought an aluminum bat, it was $300. So, I don't think it has been anything intentional on the part of Perfect Game.

Dan: This is purely hypothetical, but had your sons not been involved with Perfect Game, do you think they would have been drafted as high as they were?

Manny: Yes, because they went to other major league events. Also, I had a relationship with some scouts since I was a scout with the White Sox and Kansas City Royals, so I wouldn't be a good answer for you on that.

Dan: Do you think the competition your sons faced at Perfect Game events helped prepare them for minor league baseball and eventually the major leagues?

Manny: Absolutely, because a lot of the kids they played against got drafted. I think Perfect Game prepares you for that next level of competition. Now, it's not as good as minor league baseball, but it takes you to another level. It gets you closer to minor league baseball because of the competition. You can't get that in high school baseball. Very rarely will you face a guy throwing ninety-plus in any high school setting, and you will see a guy throwing ninety-plus probably every time you hit at a Perfect Game event.

Epilogue: What a Journey

I decided to write this book because of three experiences in baseball, all with my son, Mike. The first was when we decided to get the heck out of Little League baseball. He had played at the Fort Wayne St. Joseph Little League from T-ball up until he was ten, and, finally fed up with all the politics, cliques and negativism that went on continually in the league, Mike decided he wanted to play ball at the local AABA league at Wallen so we went out and signed up. We kept hearing how different and how much better it was.

It was. The difference between the two levels was refreshing, to say the least. Not only did they play at "regular" distances, with "regular" baseball rules (you could actually take a lead off first base before the pitcher threw the ball, for instance), there was virtually none of the vicious politics we'd experienced at St. Joe, and the level of play was measurably better. These kids could play some ball! There wasn't a team at St. Joe who could compete with the teams at Wallen.

It was a great experience. None of that "machine-pitch" or any of the other nonsense of Little League. Kids could actually catch a fly ball and snag a grounder and you saw very few lob throws to the bases. Coaches weren't allowed to coach their own sons and that alone made it a great experience.

The second experience was when we graduated to travel and select ball when Mike made the Indy Bandits. That was another big step. The level of ability increased tenfold. We were beginning to experience a different brand of baseball entirely from Little League. In his first year as an eleven-year-old on the Bandits, he played almost 120 games against teams mostly from Cincinnati and Indianapolis, while his old Little League teammates were still playing 16 games and done for the summer.

The third experience was the biggest eye-opener as to what was possible in baseball. When Mike was an eighth-grader, he was spotted by Aaron Puffer, a professional scout, unknown to either of us. I only found this out last year as Mr. Puffer had never contacted us or told us he'd recommended

Mike to Perfect Game as a result of watching him pitch a game in Cincinnati that summer.

Mike got an invitation in the mail to attend the 2004 Perfect Game Midwest Undergrad Showcase in Chicago at the University of Illinois-Circle campus. He was about to enter his freshman year of high school in a month, and he was the youngest there, competing against mostly high school juniors and a few seniors. He threw a no-hitter against some of the best high school players in the Midwest, but that wasn't the experience that made me want to write this book.

It was the level of talent on the field. For the very first time in either of our lives we saw amateur baseball played the way baseball was meant to be played. Flawlessly. There wasn't a fly ball dropped, a grounder misjudged, a throw that was anything other than a laser. For a pitcher, it was like going to heaven. You could actually pitch and know that if you induced a ground ball it was going to be fielded and the out made. Even on a pretty good select team, there were still errors. At this showcase there weren't any. Now I'm not saying every game played in a Perfect Game showcase is flawless; errors are made at these events just like any other level. Even major leaguers make errors. But we must have gotten lucky because when Mike played there were none. As we found out later after more showcase experiences, when an error happens, it's not expected. That is the opposite of the Little League and high school experiences, where errors are routine. And there were plenty of tough plays at the first showcase. The difference was, these kids made them. And you could just tell they didn't see them as hard plays or unusual plays at all — they were just routine. The entire experience was an epiphany.

These were the big boys. This was baseball as it was meant to be played. It was just a total revelation of what was possible. The field was immaculate and awe-inspiring. When you looked out from home plate to centerfield, the Sears Tower and the Chicago skyline was centered perfectly. It's like they say, "Once you've been to the city, you can't go back to the farm." Once you've played on a field like UIC's and played with the kind of talent assembled at a Perfect Game showcase, Little League just ain't ever gonna cut it again.

So how did those three experiences lead to this book? I know there are easily millions of dads and their sons who don't have a clue what's going on in this baseball world — the world of true select teams and high level showcases. People who don't realize a large and complex universe of baseball exists beyond their local Little League centerfield fence. Who think they're seeing good talent at the Little League World Series when in reality it's subpar compared to what thousands of other kids are doing. I know also there are thousands and thousands of high school coaches who are like the one I quoted early in the book as thinking that showcases are "A guy with a stopwatch who wants to make some money," and who, in their ignorance, are harming their players' chances of success at a higher level.

My intent is to not only describe the real world of youth baseball today, but beyond that, to reveal that world to the kids and their parents so they'll know how to go about realizing their dreams. There are untold millions of kids out there who just don't know what's possible.

Baseball, when played properly, is the best game ever invented. I was going to say, "in my opinion," but I'm not. You don't say "in my opinion" when something is true. It is what it is.

Like Buck O'Neil said, "You never hear anyone saying their daddies took them to their first basketball game. But you hear it all the time with baseball." Think about it. If that doesn't say baseball is the best game invented, nothing does.

I only know it has bonded Mike and me for life and that's not a bad thing at all, in my estimation.

Sources

Arp, Jim. Personal interviews, January 2004–June 2007.

Christman, Kevin. Telephone interviews by Cliff Myers, November 2007.

Clark, Roy. Personal interview by Mike and Les Edgerton, June 15, 2007.

Curtis, Charlotte. Emails, December 16, 2006.

DeJesus, Javier. Personal interviews, 2006–2008.

Dunno, Rich. Personal interviews, 2007–2008.

Edgerton, Bill. Personal interviews, 2004–2007.

Ford, Andy. Telephone interviews by Sam Clinton, December 2007.

Ford, Ben. Phone and email interviews by Sam Clinton, December 2007.

Ford, Betty. Personal interviews, January 2004–June 2008.

Ford, Jerry. Personal interviews, phone interviews, and emails, January 2004–June 2008.

Fulton, Frank. Telephone interviews by Jake Colson, November 2007.

Gerst, Jason. Phone and email interviews by Mario Ramon.

Grewe, David. Personal interview, August 2005.

Griffith, Jeff. Interviews, 2002–2004.

Hanrahan, Mark. Phone and email interviews, February 2008.

Hoop, Brian. Phone and email interviews by Mike Leyland, February 2006.

Husted, Matt. Personal interview by Mike Leyland and Les Edgerton, March 16, 2007.

Jackson, Tom. Personal interviews, 2004–2007.

Kazmir, Eddie. Phone interviews, June, 2008.

Kennedy, Dan. Personal interviews by Les Edgerton, 2006–2007; telephone interviews by Derrick Brenneman, December 2007.

Kerin, Bo. Phone interviews, 2007.

Kimm, Tyson. Phone and email interviews by Brenton Bartok, November 2007.

Koeppel, Gary. Phone interview by Stephen Kahl, November 2007.

Koerick, Tom, Jr. Personal interviews, 2004–2008.

Koerick, Tom, Sr. Personal interviews, 2004–2008.

Lain, Nancy. Personal interviews, June 2004–January 2008.

Little, Tom. Personal interview by Mike and Les Edgerton, June 2007; email interviews, February 2008.

Lubanski, Wally. Personal interview, October 2007.

McCoullough, Taylor. Phone interviews by Kara L. Benschneider, November 2007.

Maloney, David. Phone interviews, December 2005.

Mee, Corey. Personal interviews, 2005–2007.

Miller, R.W. "Bob." Telephone interviews, January 2006.

Mixon, David. Email interview by Omar A. Hosini, October 2007.

Pincus, Bob. Personal interviews, October 2007, telephone interviews, 2007–2008.

Rawnsley, David. Personal interview, October 2007.

Schrage, David. Personal interview by Mike Leyland and Les Edgerton, February 2007.

Sigfrinius, Julie. Emails, October 2006.

Simpson, Allan. Personal, email and phone interviews by Chris Wells and Les Edgerton, 2005–2007.

Thompson, Mike. Telephone and email interviews, 2007–2008.

Upton, Manny. Telephone and email interviews by Dan Higgenbotham, November 2007.

Walser, Don. Personal interviews by Les Edgerton, phone interviews and emails by Joe Clark, January 2004–June 2007.

Walsh, Joe. Phone interviews and emails, 2006–2007.

Wilhelmsen, John. Telephone interviews, January 2006.

Yasutake, Kentaro. Telephone interviews by Mitch Harshbarger, November 2007.

Index